# The *Illustrated* ATLAS *of* ARCHITECTURE

## AND MARVELOUS MONUMENTS

Sarah Tavernier and Alexandre Verhille

Translated by Noelia Hobeika

LITTLE
GESTALTEN

# CONTENTS

Atlantic Ocean

Pacific Ocean

Pacific Ocean

Atlantic Ocean

Embark on a journey to discover architects' masterpieces from around the globe and from different eras. Houses, hotels, museums, places of worship, memorials, bridges, sports fields... the world abounds with buildings whose beauty and originality are fascinating. No matter the time period, architectural geniuses have pushed the limits of what was conceived as possible, defying laws of construction and gifting us with extraordinary structures. Spot these buildings on the maps and then find more information about them in the detailed pages that follow. Enjoy!

Pacific
Ocean

Indian
Ocean

N

HALLGRÍMSKIRKJA
**13** REYKJAVÍK
*Iceland*

*Norway*

OPERA HOUSE
**7** OSLO

STAVKIRKE
HEDDAL **8**

*Sweden*

TITANIC BELFAST

THE CRYSTAL

*United Kingdom*

*North Sea*

**12** BELFAST

THE SPIRE **5**
DUBLIN
*Ireland*

*Denmark*
COPENHAGEN **6**

BERLINER FERNSEHTURM
BERLIN **4**

*Germany*

THE GHERKIN
**9** **10** **11** LONDON

THE ATOMIUM
**1** BRUSSELS
*Belgium*

LUXEMBOURG
**2** *Luxembourg*

THE DANCING HOUSE

PRAGUE
**28**
*Czech Republic*

*Atlantic Ocean*

*Nether-lands*

EIFFEL TOWER

**21** **22**
PARIS

PHILHARMONIC

NEUSCHWANSTEIN CASTLE

*France*

**3**

*Switzer-land*

VIENNA **26**
*Austria*

ST. STEPHEN'S CATHEDRAL

*Slovenia*

THE GUGGENHEIM MUSEUM **14**
BILBAO

MILLAU VIADUCT

THE DUOMO

MILAN **18**

THE TOWER OF PISA

*Croatia*

*Portugal*
*Spain*

**23**
MILLAU

PISA
**17**
*Italy*

**20** VASCO DA GAMA BRIDGE
LISBON

SAGRADA FAMILIA
BARCELONA **16**

*Monaco*

*Andorra*

ROME **19**

**15** VALENCIA
PALAU DE LES ARTS

*Mediterranean Sea*

THE COLOSSEUM

Finland

Estonia

THE CATHEDRAL OF
VASILY THE BLESSED
MOSCOW (31)(32)(33)

Latvia

Lithuania

Russia

(29) THE CROOKED
SOPOT HOUSE

Poland

(30)
WARSAW

THE PALACE OF
CULTURE AND SCIENCE

Belarus

SAINT MICHAEL'S GOLDEN-
DOMED MONASTERY
(27) KIEV

Slovakia

Ukraine

Hungary

Romania

Moldova

Bosnia and
Herzegovina

THE PALACE OF THE PARLIAMENT

(34) BUCHAREST

Black
Sea

Serbia

Bulgaria

Montenegro
Kosovo

ALEXANDER NEVSKY
CATHEDRAL

(35)
SOFIA

ISTANBUL
(36)

Macedonia

Turkey

THE BLUE MOSQUE

Albania

Greece

PARTHENÓN

KALAMBAKA

(24)

(25) ATHENS

THE METÉORA
MONASTERIES

# EUROPE

## 48 COUNTRIES

AZORES (PORTUGAL)

MOSCOW (RUSSIA)

### Europe

Also dubbed The Old Continent in contrast to
the Americas (the New World), Europe has been
exposed to many civilizations and artistic
currents throughout the centuries.
Ancient Greece, the Romans, influence from
the Byzantine Empire, Gothic art, the Renaissance,
Baroque art, Classicism, Modernism... A heritage
with rich and diverse roots that can
be witnessed in its architecture.

**729** million inhabitants

**10 %** OF THE WORLD'S POPULATION

SURFACE AREA: **4,104,265 MI²**
DENSITY: **27** PEOPLE PER SQUARE MILE

### AVERAGE TEMPERATURE

**42,8 °F** IN MOSCOW (RUSSIA)

**64,4 °F** IN ATHENS (GREECE)

# NORTHERN EUROPE

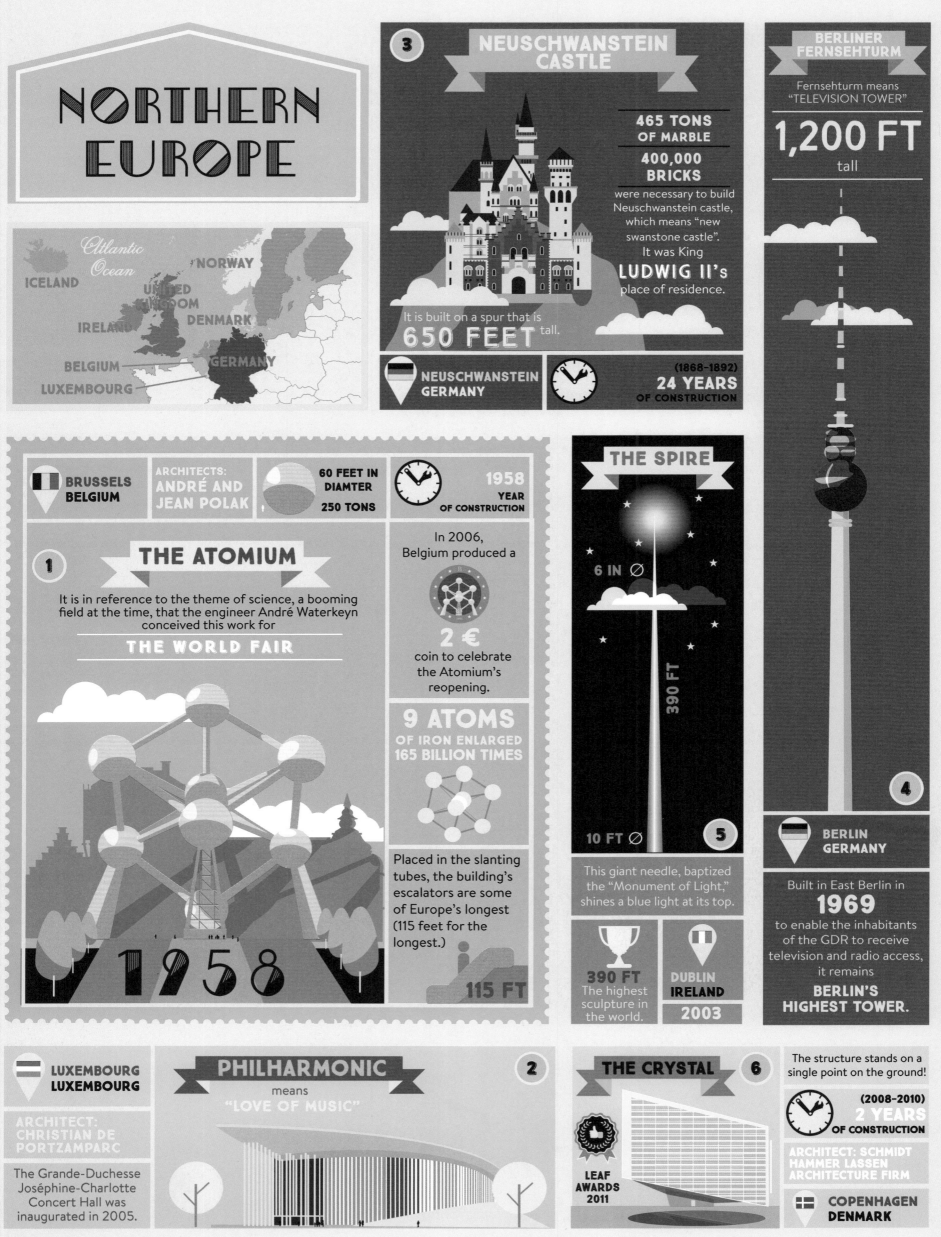

**Atlantic Ocean**

ICELAND · NORWAY · UNITED KINGDOM · IRELAND · DENMARK · BELGIUM · GERMANY · LUXEMBOURG

## 3 — NEUSCHWANSTEIN CASTLE

**465 TONS OF MARBLE**

**400,000 BRICKS**

were necessary to build Neuschwanstein castle, which means "new swanstone castle". It was King **LUDWIG II's** place of residence.

It is built on a spur that is **650 FEET** tall.

NEUSCHWANSTEIN GERMANY

**(1868–1892) 24 YEARS OF CONSTRUCTION**

## BERLINER FERNSEHTURM

Fernsehturm means "TELEVISION TOWER"

**1,200 FT** tall

## 1 — THE ATOMIUM

BRUSSELS BELGIUM

ARCHITECTS: ANDRÉ AND JEAN POLAK

**60 FEET IN DIAMTER**
**250 TONS**

**1958 YEAR OF CONSTRUCTION**

It is in reference to the theme of science, a booming field at the time, that the engineer André Waterkeyn conceived this work for **THE WORLD FAIR**

In 2006, Belgium produced a **2 €** coin to celebrate the Atomium's reopening.

**9 ATOMS OF IRON ENLARGED 165 BILLION TIMES**

Placed in the slanting tubes, the building's escalators are some of Europe's longest (115 feet for the longest.)

**115 FT**

**1958**

## THE SPIRE

**6 IN ⌀**

**390 FT**

**10 FT ⌀**

5

This giant needle, baptized the "Monument of Light," shines a blue light at its top.

**390 FT** The highest sculpture in the world.

**DUBLIN IRELAND 2003**

## 4 — BERLIN GERMANY

Built in East Berlin in **1969** to enable the inhabitants of the GDR to receive television and radio access, it remains **BERLIN'S HIGHEST TOWER.**

## 2 — PHILHARMONIC

means "LOVE OF MUSIC"

LUXEMBOURG LUXEMBOURG

ARCHITECT: CHRISTIAN DE PORTZAMPARC

The Grande-Duchesse Joséphine-Charlotte Concert Hall was inaugurated in 2005.

## 6 — THE CRYSTAL

The structure stands on a single point on the ground!

**(2008–2010) 2 YEARS OF CONSTRUCTION**

ARCHITECT: SCHMIDT HAMMER LASSEN ARCHITECTURE FIRM

COPENHAGEN DENMARK

**LEAF AWARDS 2011**

# OSLO OPERA HOUSE

**7**

WINNER OF THE
**MIES VAN DER ROHE**
PRIZE IN 2009

**ARCHITECT:**
**SNØHETTA ARCHITECTS**

**OSLO NORWAY**

(2003-2008)
**5 YEARS**
OF CONSTRUCTION

---

# STAVKIRKE

**8**

**THE BIGGEST STAVE CHURCH IN NORWAY**

ENTIRELY MADE WITH **SCOTS PINE.**

**HEDDAL NORWAY**

**13ᵀᴴ CENTURY** PERIOD OF CONSTRUCTION

---

# THE GHERKIN

**9**

**30 ST MARY AXE**
Londoners gave the building its nickname because of its shape.

**2003 EMPORIS SKYSCRAPER AWARD**

Prize for the most remarkable skyscraper in the world.

**1ˢᵀ ECOLOGICAL SKYSCRAPER**

Thanks to its **AERODYNAMIC** shape, it maximizes daylight as a source of energy.

(2001-2003)
**2 YEARS** OF CONSTRUCTION

**ARCHITECT: NORMAN FOSTER**

**LONDON UNITED KINGDOM**

---

# BIG BEN

**10**

## DID YOU KNOW?
Only UK residents are allowed to visit **BIG BEN**!

**BIG BEN** is first and foremost the nickname of **THE BELL** within the **CLOCK-TOWER**, which is also referred to as the Elizabeth tower to pay homage to the **QUEEN**.

Weight: 13.5 tons
Height: 7 feet
Diameter: 8.85 feet

**LONDON UNITED KINGDOM**

(1843-1859)
**16 YEARS** OF CONSTRUCTION

---

# THE SHARD

**11**

**1,100 FT**

**1,010 FT**

**THE LITTLE SISTER OF THE MERCURY CITY TOWER IN MOSCOW.**

Nº **69** AND **72**

On the 69th and 72nd floors, visitors can enjoy a panoramic view of London. When the weather is nice, you can see as far as 40 miles away!

It towers above all other buildings in London

**590 FT**

**315 FT**

**LONDON UNITED KINGDOM**

**ARCHITECT: RENZO PIANO**

(2008-2012)
**4 YEARS** OF CONSTRUCTION

---

# TITANIC BELFAST

**12**

This building was constructed to pay homage to the **TITANIC** which sank in April 1912. It is located on the site of the former shipyard where the Titanic was built.

**TITANIC**

**3,000** aluminum panels cover the building.

(2009-2012)
**3 YEARS** OF CONSTRUCTION

**BELFAST UNITED KINGDOM**

**REYKJAVÍK ICELAND**

**ARCHITECT: GUÐJÓN SAMÚELSSON**

(1945-1989)
**44 YEARS** OF CONSTRUCTION

---

# HALLGRÍMSKIRKJA

**13**

There are **5,200 PIPES** in the organ of the church.

Its architecture is reminiscent of **BASALTIC ORGANS.**

# SOUTHERN EUROPE

*Atlantic Ocean*

PORTUGAL
FRANCE
SPAIN
ITALY
GREECE

## 14 · THE GUGGENHEIM MUSEUM

During his career, Frank Gehry received numerous prizes, including the

**PRITZKER PRIZE**

which is the highest distinction an architect can receive.

CONTEMPORARY ART MUSEUM

BILBAO SPAIN

ARCHITECT: FRANK GEHRY

(1993–1997)
**4 YEARS** OF CONSTRUCTION

## THE TOWER OF PISA · 17

This tower is famous for leaning toward the south. In 2013, 10 years after it had undergone stability restorations, the tower had naturally straightened itself by 1 inch! Its current inclination of 3.99°.

**190 FEET HIGH**
**17 FEET OF DEVIATION**

between the peak and the vertical gradient (at its maximum in 1993!)

(1173–1372)
**199 YEARS** OF CONSTRUCTION

PISA ITALY

**3.99°** angle of inclination

## THE DUOMO · 18

The Duomo in Milan is

**THE 2ND LARGEST**

Gothic cathedral in the world. Despite a construction time of over six centuries, it kept a unified style.

## THE FAÇADE
IN A FEW NUMBERS

**250** statues
**47** low reliefs
**220** feet in width
**185** feet in height

**96** gargoyles
**135** spires

**350 FT** maximum height

**3,400** statues

(1386–1965)
**579 YEARS** OF CONSTRUCTION

MILAN ITALY

## THE COLOSSEUM · 19

**THE BIGGEST ROMAN AMPHITEATER EVER TO BE CONSTRUCTED**

**SEATING CAPACITY: 50,000 TO 75,000 PEOPLE**
For 500 years, the Colosseum hosted gladiator fights, shows and wild animal hunts. During the inauguration, 9,000 animals were sacrificed.

ROME ITALY

(70–80 A.D.)
**10 YEARS** OF CONSTRUCTION

Style: Roman

## PALACE OF THE ARTS
### REINA SOFÍA

**OPERA**

CENTER FOR MUSIC AND PERFORMING ARTS

### 15

(1996–2005)
**9 YEARS** OF CONSTRUCTION

VALENCIA SPAIN

ARCHITECT: SANTIAGO CALATRAVA

## EXPIATORY TEMPLE OF THE
### SAGRADA FAMILIA · 16

### ANTONI GAUDÍ

Gaudí dedicated his life to the erection of this edifice. He died in 1926, before construction was finished. Since it is an expiatory temple, construction is entirely financed by donations and visitor entrance fees. The end of construction is planned for 2026 to coincide with the centenary anniversary of Gaudí's death.

BARCELONA SPAIN

(1882–2026)
**144 YEARS** OF CONSTRUCTION

**UNESCO** World Heritage Site

### PARK GÜELL

It was meant to be a garden town with 60 houses and a chapel. Due to the cost of construction, which stopped in 1914, only 3 houses were completed.

ARCHITECT: FOSTER & PARTNERS

MILLAU FRANCE

(2001–2004)
**3 YEARS** OF CONSTRUCTION

**RECORD-BREAKING BRIDGE**

### MILLAU VIADUCT · 23

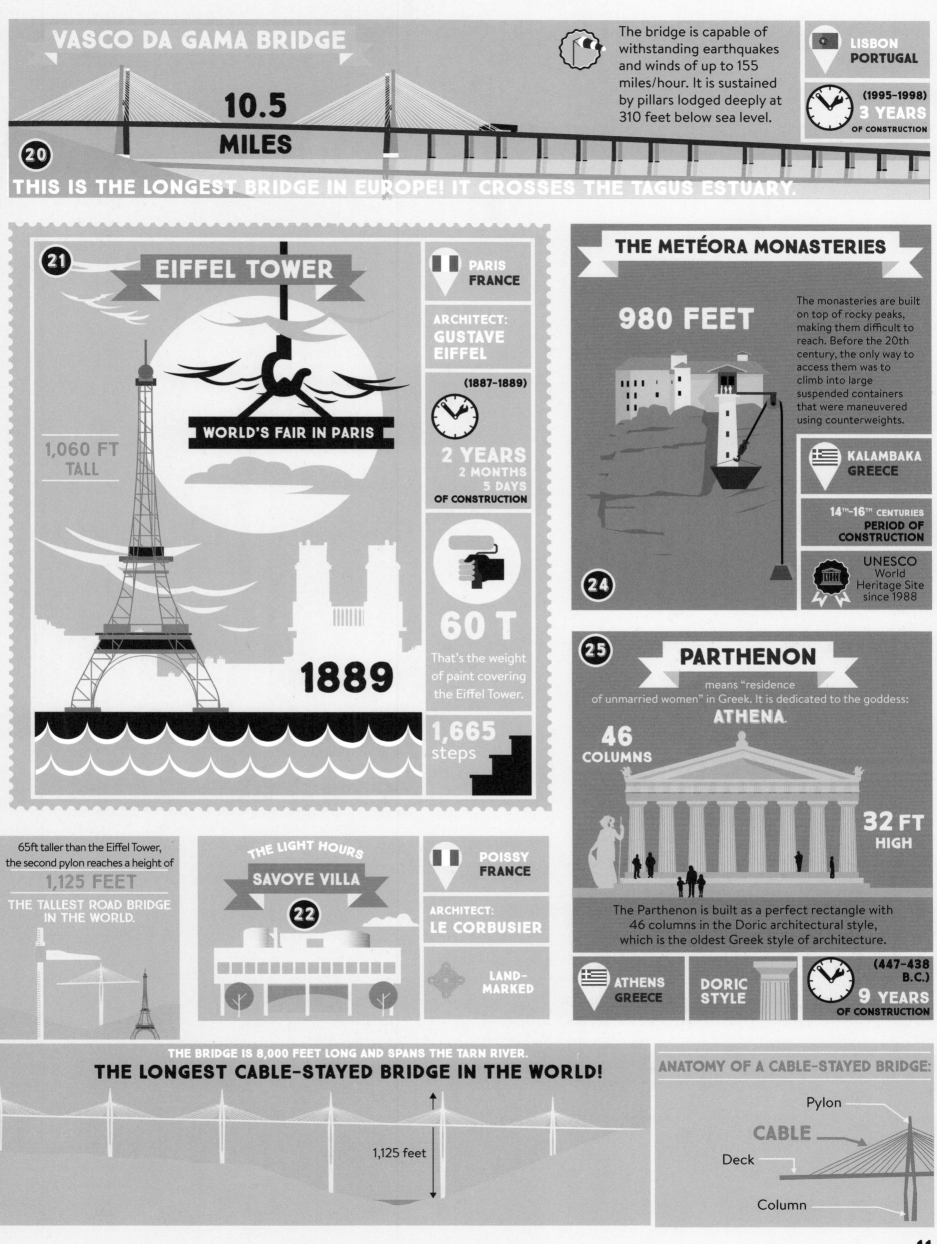

## VASCO DA GAMA BRIDGE

**20**

### 10.5 MILES

The bridge is capable of withstanding earthquakes and winds of up to 155 miles/hour. It is sustained by pillars lodged deeply at 310 feet below sea level.

**LISBON PORTUGAL**

**(1995-1998) 3 YEARS OF CONSTRUCTION**

**THIS IS THE LONGEST BRIDGE IN EUROPE! IT CROSSES THE TAGUS ESTUARY.**

---

**21**

## EIFFEL TOWER

**PARIS FRANCE**

**ARCHITECT: GUSTAVE EIFFEL**

**(1887-1889)**

**2 YEARS 2 MONTHS 5 DAYS OF CONSTRUCTION**

WORLD'S FAIR IN PARIS

1,060 FT TALL

**1889**

**60 T**
That's the weight of paint covering the Eiffel Tower.

**1,665 steps**

---

## THE METÉORA MONASTERIES

**980 FEET**

The monasteries are built on top of rocky peaks, making them difficult to reach. Before the 20th century, the only way to access them was to climb into large suspended containers that were maneuvered using counterweights.

**KALAMBAKA GREECE**

**14ᵀᴴ-16ᵀᴴ CENTURIES PERIOD OF CONSTRUCTION**

**UNESCO World Heritage Site since 1988**

**24**

---

**25**

## PARTHENON

means "residence of unmarried women" in Greek. It is dedicated to the goddess: **ATHENA**.

**46 COLUMNS**

**32 FT HIGH**

The Parthenon is built as a perfect rectangle with 46 columns in the Doric architectural style, which is the oldest Greek style of architecture.

**ATHENS GREECE**

**DORIC STYLE**

**(447-438 B.C.) 9 YEARS OF CONSTRUCTION**

---

65ft taller than the Eiffel Tower, the second pylon reaches a height of
**1,125 FEET**
THE TALLEST ROAD BRIDGE IN THE WORLD.

### THE LIGHT HOURS
## SAVOYE VILLA

**22**

**POISSY FRANCE**

**ARCHITECT: LE CORBUSIER**

**LAND-MARKED**

---

**THE BRIDGE IS 8,000 FEET LONG AND SPANS THE TARN RIVER.**
## THE LONGEST CABLE-STAYED BRIDGE IN THE WORLD!

1,125 feet

### ANATOMY OF A CABLE-STAYED BRIDGE:

Pylon

**CABLE**

Deck

Column

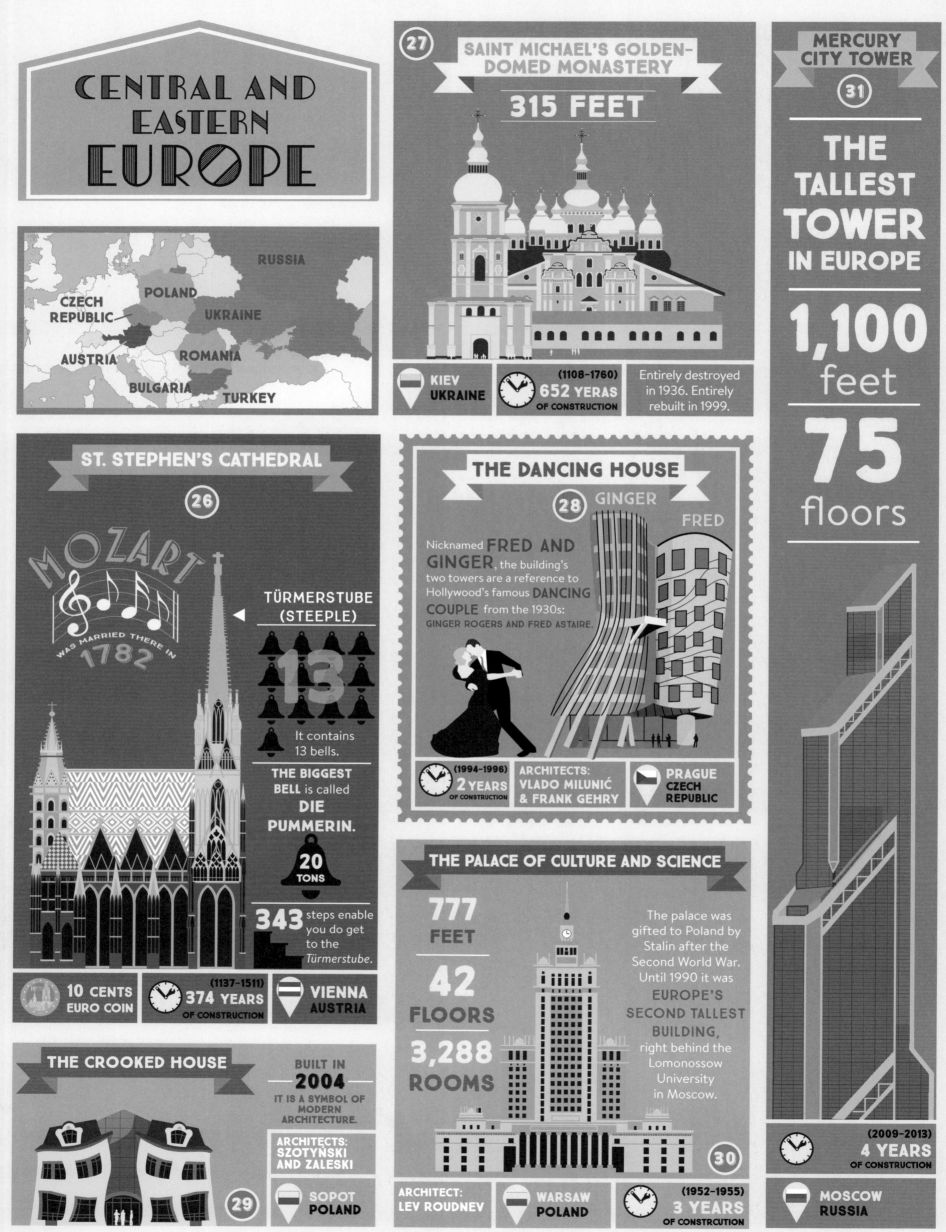

# CENTRAL AND EASTERN EUROPE

RUSSIA
POLAND
CZECH REPUBLIC
UKRAINE
AUSTRIA
ROMANIA
BULGARIA
TURKEY

## SAINT MICHAEL'S GOLDEN-DOMED MONASTERY

**27**

### 315 FEET

KIEV UKRAINE

(1108–1760) **652 YERAS** OF CONSTRUCTION

Entirely destroyed in 1936. Entirely rebuilt in 1999.

## MERCURY CITY TOWER

**31**

### THE TALLEST TOWER IN EUROPE

### 1,100 feet

### 75 floors

(2009–2013) **4 YEARS** OF CONSTRUCTION

MOSCOW RUSSIA

## ST. STEPHEN'S CATHEDRAL

**26**

MOZART WAS MARRIED THERE IN 1782

### TÜRMERSTUBE (STEEPLE)

### 13

It contains 13 bells.

**THE BIGGEST BELL** is called **DIE PUMMERIN.**

### 20 TONS

### 343 steps enable you do get to the Türmerstube.

10 CENTS EURO COIN

(1137–1511) **374 YEARS** OF CONSTRUCTION

VIENNA AUSTRIA

## THE DANCING HOUSE

**28**

GINGER

FRED

Nicknamed **FRED AND GINGER**, the building's two towers are a reference to Hollywood's famous **DANCING COUPLE** from the 1930s: GINGER ROGERS AND FRED ASTAIRE.

(1994–1996) **2 YEARS** OF CONSTRUCTION

ARCHITECTS: VLADO MILUNIĆ & FRANK GEHRY

PRAGUE CZECH REPUBLIC

## THE PALACE OF CULTURE AND SCIENCE

### 777 FEET

### 42 FLOORS

### 3,288 ROOMS

The palace was gifted to Poland by Stalin after the Second World War. Until 1990 it was **EUROPE'S SECOND TALLEST BUILDING,** right behind the Lomonossow University in Moscow.

**30**

ARCHITECT: LEV ROUDNEV

WARSAW POLAND

(1952–1955) **3 YEARS** OF CONSTRUCTION

## THE CROOKED HOUSE

BUILT IN **2004**

IT IS A SYMBOL OF MODERN ARCHITECTURE.

ARCHITECTS: SZOTYŃSKI AND ZALESKI

**29**

SOPOT POLAND

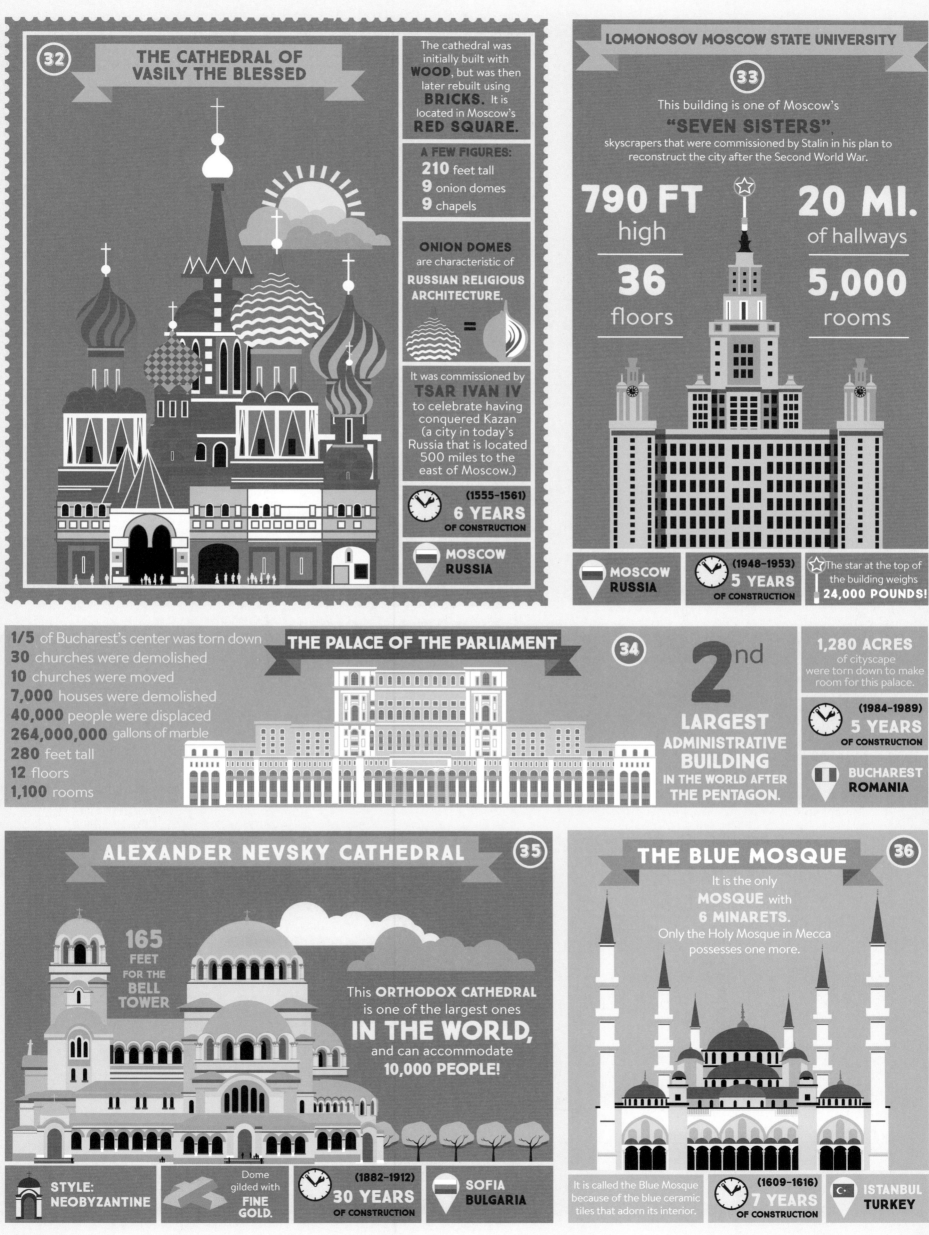

## THE CATHEDRAL OF VASILY THE BLESSED

**32**

The cathedral was initially built with **WOOD**, but was then later rebuilt using **BRICKS**. It is located in Moscow's **RED SQUARE**.

**A FEW FIGURES:**
**210** feet tall
**9** onion domes
**9** chapels

**ONION DOMES** are characteristic of **RUSSIAN RELIGIOUS ARCHITECTURE.**

It was commissioned by **TSAR IVAN IV** to celebrate having conquered Kazan (a city in today's Russia that is located 500 miles to the east of Moscow.)

(1555–1561)
**6 YEARS** OF CONSTRUCTION

**MOSCOW RUSSIA**

## LOMONOSOV MOSCOW STATE UNIVERSITY

**33**

This building is one of Moscow's **"SEVEN SISTERS"**, skyscrapers that were commissioned by Stalin in his plan to reconstruct the city after the Second World War.

**790 FT** high
**20 MI.** of hallways
**36** floors
**5,000** rooms

**MOSCOW RUSSIA**

(1948–1953)
**5 YEARS** OF CONSTRUCTION

The star at the top of the building weighs **24,000 POUNDS!**

## THE PALACE OF THE PARLIAMENT

**34**

**1/5** of Bucharest's center was torn down
**30** churches were demolished
**10** churches were moved
**7,000** houses were demolished
**40,000** people were displaced
**264,000,000** gallons of marble
**280** feet tall
**12** floors
**1,100** rooms

**2**nd **LARGEST ADMINISTRATIVE BUILDING** IN THE WORLD AFTER **THE PENTAGON.**

**1,280 ACRES** of cityscape were torn down to make room for this palace.

(1984–1989)
**5 YEARS** OF CONSTRUCTION

**BUCHAREST ROMANIA**

## ALEXANDER NEVSKY CATHEDRAL

**35**

**165** FEET FOR THE **BELL TOWER**

This **ORTHODOX CATHEDRAL** is one of the largest ones **IN THE WORLD,** and can accommodate **10,000 PEOPLE!**

**STYLE: NEOBYZANTINE**

Dome gilded with **FINE GOLD.**

(1882–1912)
**30 YEARS** OF CONSTRUCTION

**SOFIA BULGARIA**

## THE BLUE MOSQUE

**36**

It is the only **MOSQUE** with **6 MINARETS.** Only the Holy Mosque in Mecca possesses one more.

It is called the Blue Mosque because of the blue ceramic tiles that adorn its interior.

(1609–1616)
**7 YEARS** OF CONSTRUCTION

**ISTANBUL TURKEY**

CASABLANCA **1**

AMPHITEATER
OF EL DJEM

**2** EL DJEM

*Tunisia*

*Morocco*

MELIKA **5**

**3**

HASSAN II MOSQUE

QASR AL-HAJ

SHEIKH SIDI AÏSSA
MAUSOLEUM

QASR AL-HAJ

*Libya*

*Mauritania*

*Mali*

*Algeria*

*Niger*

*Chad*

AFRICAN
RENAISSANCE
MONUMENT

GREAT MOSQUE
**DJENNÉ**

NATIONAL
HEROES
MEMORIAL

*Cape Verde*

*Senegal*

DAKAR **10**

**4**

*Burkina
Faso*

**9** OUAGADOUGOU

*Central
African
Republic*

BANJUL **8**

AIRPORT

*Nigeria*

*Gambia*

*Benin*

BIDC BANK

*Guinea-Bissau*

*Guinea*

*Sierra Leone*

BASILICA OF OUR LADY OF PEACE

**YAMOUSSOUKRO** **11**

*Ghana*

ACCRA **7** **6**

REUNIFICATION
MONUMENT
**YAOUNDÉ**

*Liberia*

**LOMÉ**

*Togo*

**35**

*Cameroon*

*Ivory Coast*

*Equatorial
Guinea*

*Congo*

NATIONAL THEATER

*São Tomé and Príncipe*

*Gabon*

*Democratic
Republic of
Congo*

**27** KISANTU

CATHEDRAL OF OUR LADY
OF SEVEN SORROWS

*Atlantic
Ocean*

*Angola*

*Namibia*

WINDHOEK
**34**

SUPREME COURT

*Botswana*

GREEN POINT STADIUM

CAPE TOWN **33**

*South
Africa*

EL FERDAN
RAILWAY BRIDGE
*Syria*
*Lebanon*
*Israel*
DOME OF
THE ROCK

SUEZ CANAL
⑲ ⑳ ㉑ JERUSALEM
*Jordan* *Iraq* *Kuwait*

⑮ PETRA
⑬ ⑭ ⑱
GIZA
KING FAHD CAUSEWAY
BURJ KHALIFA

*Egypt*
⑫
LUXOR
THE SPHINX
AL KHAZNEH
JASRA ⑯ *Qatar* ㉔ DUBAI
*Bahrain* ㉓ ABU DHABI

MECCA
㉒
*Saudi*
*Arabia*
*Oman*

COLOSSI OF MEMNON
*Sudan*
NUBIAN
PYRAMIDS
MASJID AL-HARAM
CAPITAL GATE

*Eritrea* *Yemen*
*United*
*Arab*
*Emirates*

MEROE ⑰
GONDER ㉖ LALIBELA
㉕
*Djibouti*

*South*
*Sudan*
FASILIDES' CASTLE
SAINT-
GEORGE
CHURCH

*Ethiopia*
*Uganda*
*Somalia*
*Kenya*

*Indian*
*Ocean*

*Rwanda*
*Burundi*
*Tanzania*
*Seychelles*

⑲ ㉚ KILWA KISIWANI
THE FORT

*Mayotte (France)*
*Mozambique* *Comoros*
THE QUEEN'S PALACE

*Zambia*

*Zimbabwe*
*Malawi*
ANTANANARIVO ㉘
*Mauritius*

*Madagascar*
*Réunion*
*(France)*

CARLTON
CENTRE
㉛ *Swaziland*
JOHANNESBURG
SCULPTURE
OF NELSON
MANDELA
㉜ HOWICK
*Lesotho*

---

# AFRICA AND THE NEAR EAST

**67 COUNTRIES**

**PRAIA (CAPE VERDE)** | **MUSCAT (OMAN)**

## Africa

Africa, the cradle of civilization, is a continent that has shaped architecture throughout the centuries. In the Mediterranean basin you'll find Egyptian, Greek, Roman and Phoenician influences as you would in Southern Europe, but also a great tradition of adobe constructions that, in the Near East, stand alongside the biggest buildings in the world.

**1,290** million inhabitants | **17.5 %** OF THE WORLD'S POPULATION

SURFACE AREA: **13,270,000 MI²**
DENSITY: **14** PEOPLE PER SQUARE MILE

### AVERAGE TEMPERATURE

**62 °F** IN CAPE TOWN (SOUTH AFRICA) | **85°F** IN DJIBOUTI (DJIBOUTI)

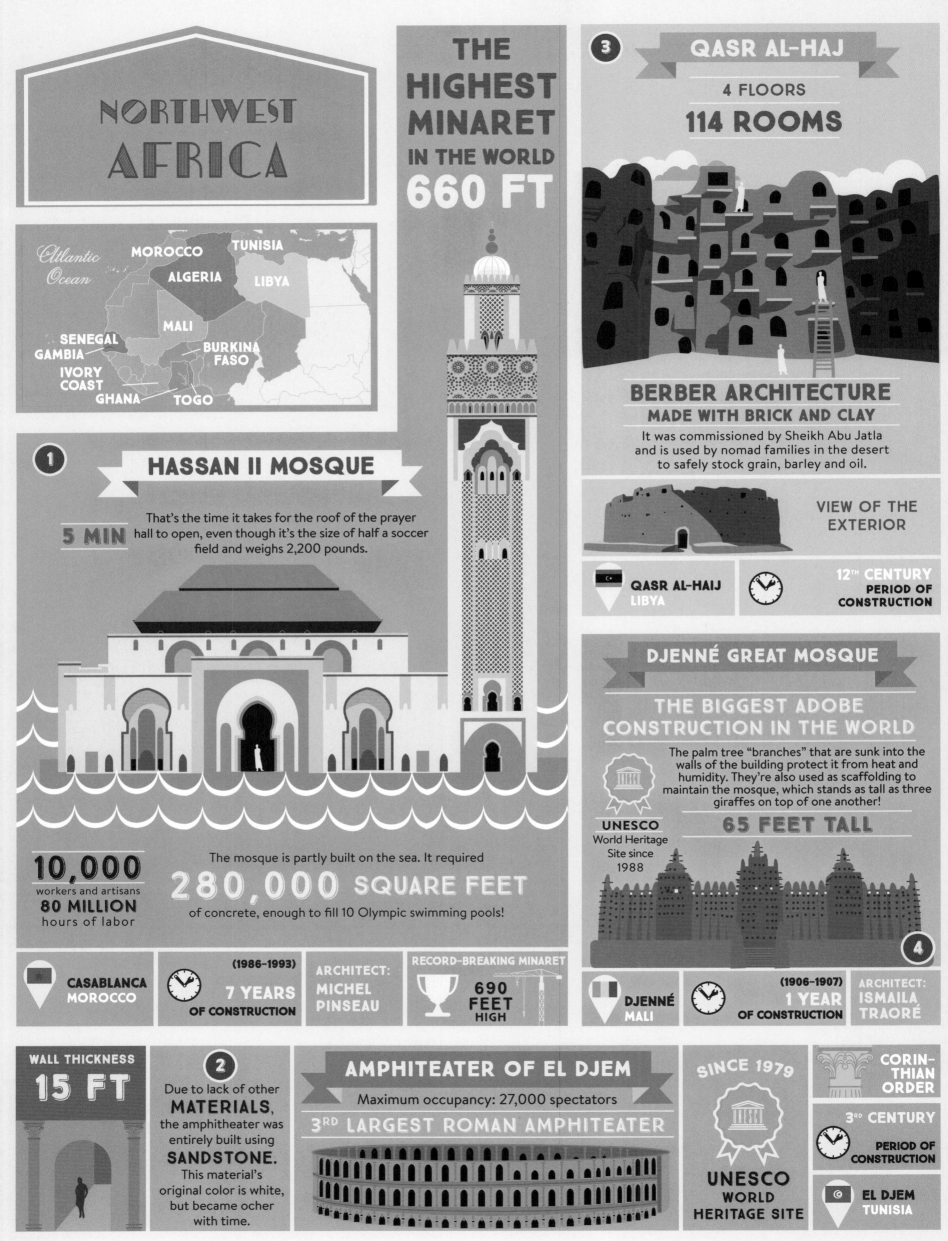

# NORTHWEST AFRICA

Atlantic Ocean

MOROCCO · TUNISIA · ALGERIA · LIBYA · MALI · SENEGAL · GAMBIA · BURKINA FASO · IVORY COAST · GHANA · TOGO

## THE HIGHEST MINARET IN THE WORLD
### 660 FT

## ③ QASR AL-HAJ
### 4 FLOORS
### 114 ROOMS

### BERBER ARCHITECTURE
### MADE WITH BRICK AND CLAY

It was commissioned by Sheikh Abu Jatla and is used by nomad families in the desert to safely stock grain, barley and oil.

VIEW OF THE EXTERIOR

QASR AL-HAIJ
LIBYA

12TH CENTURY
PERIOD OF CONSTRUCTION

## ① HASSAN II MOSQUE

**5 MIN** — That's the time it takes for the roof of the prayer hall to open, even though it's the size of half a soccer field and weighs 2,200 pounds.

**10,000** workers and artisans
**80 MILLION** hours of labor

The mosque is partly built on the sea. It required
### 280,000 SQUARE FEET
of concrete, enough to fill 10 Olympic swimming pools!

CASABLANCA MOROCCO

(1986–1993)
**7 YEARS** OF CONSTRUCTION

ARCHITECT: MICHEL PINSEAU

RECORD-BREAKING MINARET
**690 FEET HIGH**

## DJENNÉ GREAT MOSQUE

### THE BIGGEST ADOBE CONSTRUCTION IN THE WORLD

The palm tree "branches" that are sunk into the walls of the building protect it from heat and humidity. They're also used as scaffolding to maintain the mosque, which stands as tall as three giraffes on top of one another!

UNESCO World Heritage Site since 1988

### 65 FEET TALL

DJENNÉ MALI

(1906–1907)
**1 YEAR** OF CONSTRUCTION

ARCHITECT: ISMAILA TRAORÉ

④

**WALL THICKNESS**
### 15 FT

## ② 
Due to lack of other **MATERIALS**, the amphitheater was entirely built using **SANDSTONE**. This material's original color is white, but became ocher with time.

## AMPHITEATER OF EL DJEM
Maximum occupancy: 27,000 spectators
### 3RD LARGEST ROMAN AMPHITEATER

SINCE 1979
UNESCO WORLD HERITAGE SITE

CORINTHIAN ORDER

3RD CENTURY
PERIOD OF CONSTRUCTION

EL DJEM TUNISIA

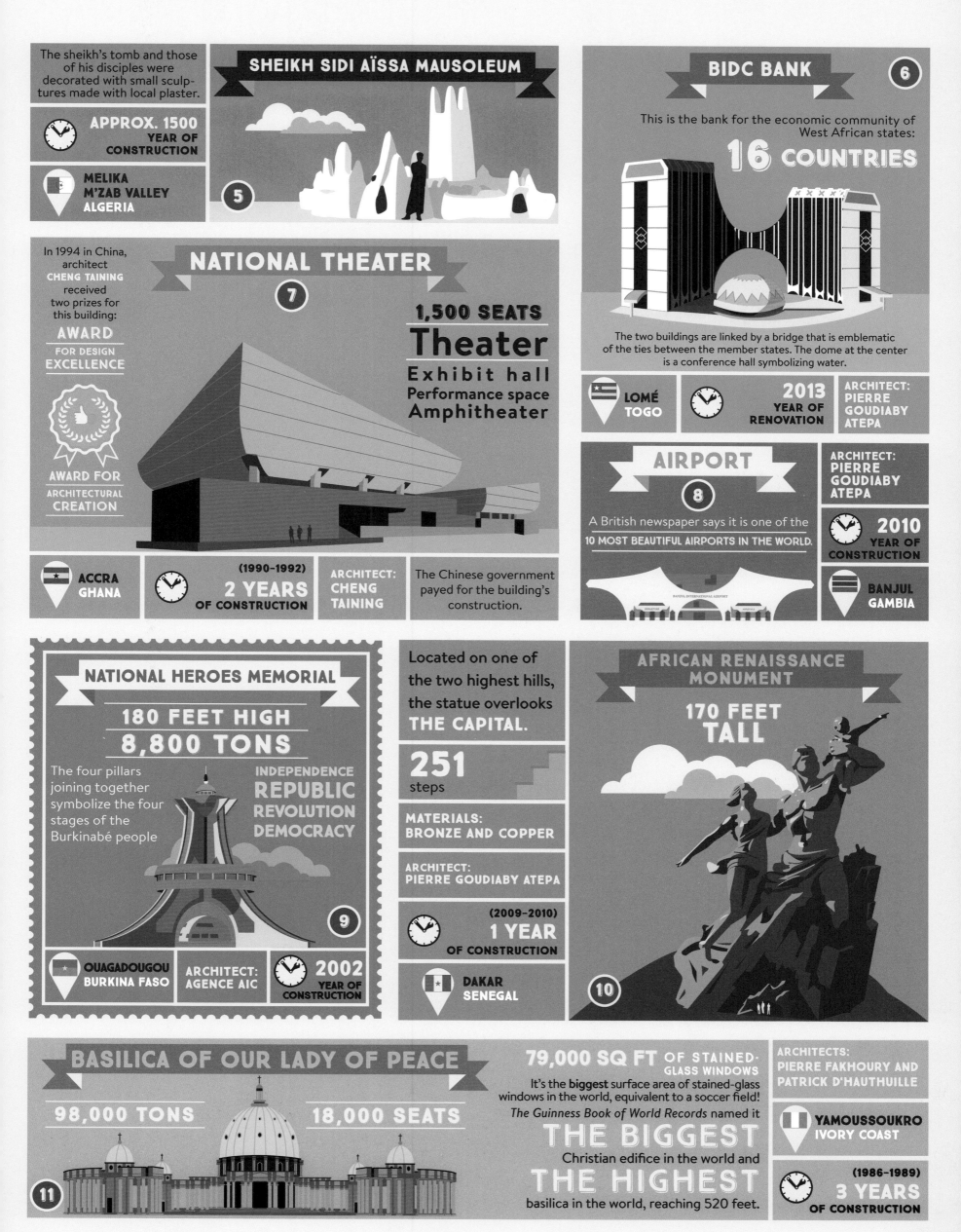

## SHEIKH SIDI AÏSSA MAUSOLEUM

The sheikh's tomb and those of his disciples were decorated with small sculptures made with local plaster.

APPROX. 1500 YEAR OF CONSTRUCTION

MELIKA M'ZAB VALLEY ALGERIA

⑤

## BIDC BANK ⑥

This is the bank for the economic community of West African states:

16 COUNTRIES

The two buildings are linked by a bridge that is emblematic of the ties between the member states. The dome at the center is a conference hall symbolizing water.

LOMÉ TOGO

2013 YEAR OF RENOVATION

ARCHITECT: PIERRE GOUDIABY ATEPA

## NATIONAL THEATER ⑦

In 1994 in China, architect CHENG TAINING received two prizes for this building:

AWARD FOR DESIGN EXCELLENCE

AWARD FOR ARCHITECTURAL CREATION

1,500 SEATS
Theater
Exhibit hall
Performance space
Amphitheater

ACCRA GHANA

(1990-1992) 2 YEARS OF CONSTRUCTION

ARCHITECT: CHENG TAINING

The Chinese government payed for the building's construction.

## AIRPORT ⑧

A British newspaper says it is one of the 10 MOST BEAUTIFUL AIRPORTS IN THE WORLD.

BANJUL INTERNATIONAL AIRPORT

ARCHITECT: PIERRE GOUDIABY ATEPA

2010 YEAR OF CONSTRUCTION

BANJUL GAMBIA

## NATIONAL HEROES MEMORIAL

180 FEET HIGH
8,800 TONS

The four pillars joining together symbolize the four stages of the Burkinabé people

INDEPENDENCE
REPUBLIC
REVOLUTION
DEMOCRACY

OUAGADOUGOU BURKINA FASO

ARCHITECT: AGENCE AIC

2002 YEAR OF CONSTRUCTION

⑨

Located on one of the two highest hills, the statue overlooks THE CAPITAL.

251 steps

MATERIALS: BRONZE AND COPPER

ARCHITECT: PIERRE GOUDIABY ATEPA

(2009-2010) 1 YEAR OF CONSTRUCTION

DAKAR SENEGAL

## AFRICAN RENAISSANCE MONUMENT

170 FEET TALL

⑩

## BASILICA OF OUR LADY OF PEACE

98,000 TONS

18,000 SEATS

⑪

79,000 SQ FT OF STAINED-GLASS WINDOWS
It's the biggest surface area of stained-glass windows in the world, equivalent to a soccer field!
*The Guinness Book of World Records* named it

THE BIGGEST

Christian edifice in the world and

THE HIGHEST

basilica in the world, reaching 520 feet.

ARCHITECTS: PIERRE FAKHOURY AND PATRICK D'HAUTHUILLE

YAMOUSSOUKRO IVORY COAST

(1986-1989) 3 YEARS OF CONSTRUCTION

# NORTHEAST AFRICA AND THE NEAR EAST

ISRAEL · JORDAN · BAHRAIN · SAUDI ARABIA · EGYPT · SUDAN · UNITED ARAB EMIRATES

## 15 · AL KHAZNEH

AL KHAZNEH was dug out of and sculpted from RED SANDSTONE.

### AL KHAZNEH

In Arabic, Khazneh means **"PHARAOH'S TREASURE"**.
But it's not a treasure, it's **THE TOMB OF A KING.**
You can gain access to the tomb after a half-hour walk through a rocky pathway called **THE SIQ.**

**130 FEET** IS THE FAÇADE'S HEIGHT

UNESCO World Heritage Site since 1985

The façade was filmed in one of the "Indiana Jones" movies.

PETRA JORDAN

APPROX. 1ST CENTURY B.C — PERIOD OF CONSTRUCTION

## COLOSSI OF MEMNON

Back in the day, they framed the doorway into Amenhotep III's "Temple of a Million Years."

These are monumental stone sculptures that are **60 FEET TALL.**

The vestiges of the two colossi represent Amenhotep III. On either side of his legs you can find his wife Tiyi and his mother Mutemwiya.

12

LUXOR EGYPT

APPROX. 1350 B.C. YEAR OF CONSTRUCTION

## THE SPHINX

### 14

**1 MILLION HOURS** of labor to sculpt it.

**THE BIGGEST MONUMENTAL MONOLITHIC SCULPTURE IN THE WORLD**

**17 FEET TALL** just the head

The sculpture was carved straight into the block of stone and faces the Giza pyramids.

APPROX. 2500 B.C. YEAR OF CONSTRUCTION

GIZA EGYPT

## 16 · KING FAHD CAUSEWAY

GULF OF BAHRAIN

**15.5 MI**

This ensemble of bridges and embankments connects Saudi Arabia with Bahrain. It would take six hours to walk across it!

**5 BRIDGES** INTERSPERSED WITH EMBANKMENTS
**1 ARTIFICIAL ISLAND**

**12,360,000 FT³ OF CONCRETE**

(1981-1986) **5 YEARS** OF CONSTRUCTION

AL-KHOBAR SAUDI ARABIA

JASRA BAHRAIN

## 17 · NUBIAN PYRAMIDS

70° angle · 100 feet high

These are the Egyptian pyramids' cousins, but they are more pointed at the top and more modest in size. They are the mortuary monuments of the kingdom of Kush.

MEROË SUDAN

4TH CENTURY B.C.– 4TH CENTURY A.D. PERIOD OF CONSTRUCTION

UNESCO World Heritage Site since 2011

## EGYPTIAN PYRAMIDS

These are the pharaoh's tombs. Kheops' tomb is the oldest of the **7 Wonders of the Ancient World.**

**KHEOPS** The father — **KHEPHREN** The son — **MYKERINOS** The grandson

479 feet · 469 feet · 213 feet

40° angle · 750 feet

The father and son's temples were connected by a tunnel measuring **1,620 FEET.**

**RECORD-BREAKING PYRAMID**
For millennia, Kheops' pyramid was the highest, most dense, and most massive man-made construction.

GIZA EGYPT

APPROX. 2560 B.C. YEAR OF CONSTRUCTION

UNESCO World Heritage Site since 1979

The Suez Canal enables maritime trade between Europe and Asia without bypassing Africa.

**2001** YEAR OF CONSTRUCTION

ISMAILIA EGYPT

## 18 · EL FERDAN RAILWAY BRIDGE

It lets cars and trains cross the Suez Canal. The bridge opens to let boats go by.

# JERUSALEM: HOLY CITY FOR JEWS, CHRISTIANS AND MUSLIMS

JERUSALEM
ISRAEL

## CHURCH OF THE HOLY SEPULCHRE

To Christians, Holy Sepulchre means "JESUS' TOMB".

The church was built on CALVARY.

This sanctuary encompasses the place where the crucifixion took place and the cave where JESUS OF NAZARETH'S body was placed following his death.

**19**

It has been a place of pilgrimage since the 2ND CENTURY.

## WESTERN WALL

This wall is the only vestige from the temple of Jerusalem that was previously built on the site of Solomon's temple (10th century B.C.). The temple was pillaged and burned to the ground in the year 70 by the Romans.

**It is customary to write prayers onto papers that are then inserted into the stones' cracks.**

**20**

Jews consider this to be the most sacred place to pray: this is where you can find MOSES' TEN COMMANDMENTS.

**1 MILLION PILGRIMS PER YEAR**

4TH CENTURY B.C.
PERIOD OF CONSTRUCTION

The esplanade in front of the Wall is divided into three: a public area for all, a area for men, a area for women.

It is also called "Al-Buraq" by Arabs.

1ST CENTURY B.C.
PERIOD OF CONSTRUCTION

## DOME OF THE ROCK

**21**

3RD HOLY PLACE FOR MUSLIMS.

This sanctuary is home to the FOUNDATION STONE. According to Muslim tradition, this is where MUHAMMAD arrived after leaving Mecca. The dome's esplanade is supported by the Western Wall.

APPROX. 690
YEAR OF CONSTRUCTION

**82** feet high

**780 FEET**
The longest inscription from the Koran on one of the Dome's walls.

## BURJ KHALIFA

# THE TALLEST BUILDING IN THE WORLD

**11,600,000 FT³**
of concrete

**43,000 TONS**
of steel beams

**1,500,000 SQFT**
of glass

**22 MILLION**
hours of labor

**2,717** feet tall

**163** floors

The building appears in "**Mission impossible:** Ghost Protocol".

**24**

ARCHITECTS: SKIDMORE, OWINGS AND MERRILL

DUBAI
UNITED ARAB EMIRATES

(2004-2010)
**6 YEARS**
OF CONSTRUCTION

## MASJID AL-HARAM

**22**

Means "The Sacred Mosque".

### THE BIGGEST MOSQUE IN THE WORLD

**4,300,000 FT²**
That's the equivalent of 56 soccer fields.

**290** feet high

The only mosque to possess **7 MINARETS.**

**MAXIMUM CAPACITY: 900,000 PEOPLE**

**1ST HOLY PLACE FOR MUSLIMS**

MECCA
SAUDI ARABIA

(7TH–21ST CENTURY)
**1400 YEARS**
OF CONSTRUCTION

**3,000 FEET**
THE LONGEST SWING BRIDGE IN THE WORLD

## CAPITAL GATE

### THE TALLEST LEANING BUILDING IN THE WORLD

**520** feet tall

**18°** angle of inclination

**23**

ARCHITECTS: RMJM AGENCY

(2008-2010)
**2 YEARS**
OF CONSTRUCTION

ABU DHABI
UNITED ARAB EMIRATES

# CENTRAL, EASTERN AND SOUTHERN AFRICA

CAMEROON
DEMOCRATIC REPUBLIC OF CONGO
ETHIOPIA
TANZANIA
Atlantic Ocean
MADAGASCAR
NAMIBIA
SOUTH AFRICA
Indian Ocean

## THE QUEEN'S PALACE

28

4,800 FEET HIGH

### ROVA OF ANTANANARIVO

was the palace of Queen Ranavalona I. It was initially made using wood, and then rebuilt with stone.

The main pillar is a massive tree trunk of **ROSEWOOD**, which is a precious wood traditionally used in Malagasy art.

In 1995, a large fire destroyed a large part of the palace's rosewood foundations. It was restored in 2010.

### THE ROVA

designates the group of buildings that make up the royal residence:
**5 PALACES**
**1 TEMPLE**
**9 TOMBS.**

ARCHITECTS:
JEAN LABORDE
JAMES CAMERON

19TH CENTURY PERIOD OF CONSTRUCTION

ANTANANARIVO MADAGASCAR

## SAINT-GEORGE CHURCH

**120,000 FT³ OF STONE** were removed from around the church! That's the equivalent of an Olympic swimming pool!

98.5 FEET HIGH

25

What makes it interesting is that it was carved directly into the stone. It is part of an **ENSEMBLE OF 11 MONOLITHIC CHURCHES.**

It is a place of pilgrimage, especially for Orthodox Christians.

**CROSS-SHAPED**

LALIBELA ETHIOPIA

UNESCO World Heritage Site since 1978

13TH CENTURY PERIOD OF CONSTRUCTION

## FASILIDES' CASTLE

26

Built by Fasilides, the king of Ethiopia, this castle is part of a complex fortified by a

**3,000-FOOT LONG OUTER WALL WITH 12 DOORS.**

The castle is located at **7,200 FEET ABOVE SEA LEVEL** in a part of Ethiopia with lush vegetation that has attracted numerous kings. It is surrounded by other castles and churches, has several stables, a sauna, and even a place for domesticated lions!

GONDAR ETHIOPIA

17TH CENTURY PERIOD OF CONSTRUCTION

UNESCO World Heritage Site since 1979

## THE FORT

**13TH AND 14TH CENTURIES**
Apex of prosperity in Kilwa, a city off the coast of present-day Tanzania.

In the 14th century, it controlled trade in the Indian Ocean with the Arabian Peninsula, India, and China. You could trade

**GOLD AND IVORY**

for money, perfumes, earthenware and Chinese porcelain.

29

The **PORTUGUESE** constructed a fort in Kilwa during the 16th century.

## THE GREAT MOSQUE

30

**THE OLDEST MOSQUE** to be found on the East African coast.

The Kilwa sultanate was the most important one in

## SWAHILI CULTURE

(pertaining to the coastal regions of Eastern Africa).

KISANTU DEMOCRATIC REPUBLIC OF CONGO

UNESCO World Heritage Site since 1981

(1926–1936) **10 YEARS** OF CONSTRUCTION

11TH CENTURY PERIOD OF CONSTRUCTION

STYLE: NEO-ROMAN

KILWA ARCHIPELAGO TANZANIA

## CATHEDRAL OF OUR LADY OF SEVEN SORROWS

27

It can accommodate up to **4,000** people!

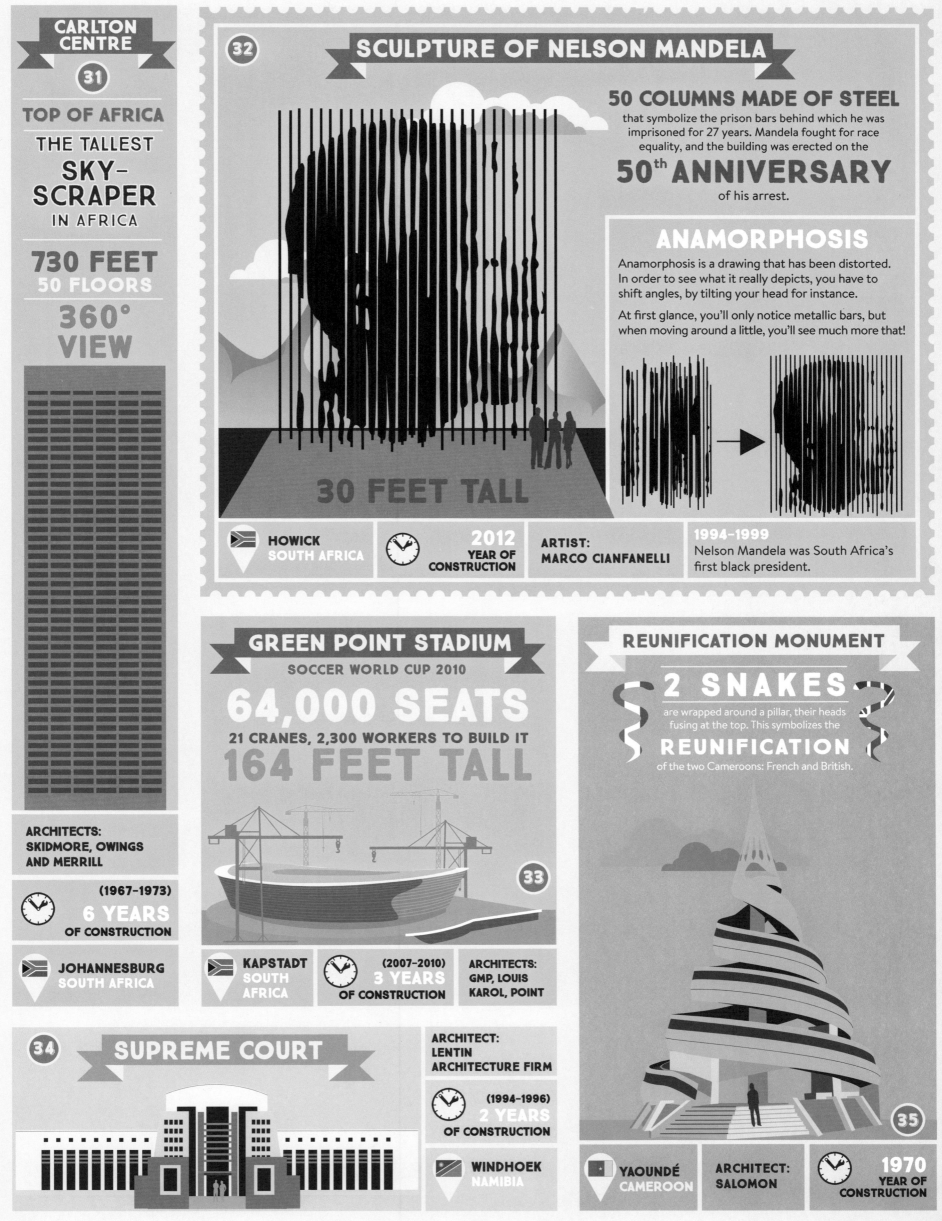

## CARLTON CENTRE

**31**

### TOP OF AFRICA

### THE TALLEST SKY-SCRAPER IN AFRICA

### 730 FEET
50 FLOORS

### 360° VIEW

**ARCHITECTS:**
**SKIDMORE, OWINGS AND MERRILL**

(1967-1973)
**6 YEARS**
OF CONSTRUCTION

**JOHANNESBURG**
SOUTH AFRICA

## SCULPTURE OF NELSON MANDELA

**32**

### 50 COLUMNS MADE OF STEEL
that symbolize the prison bars behind which he was imprisoned for 27 years. Mandela fought for race equality, and the building was erected on the

### 50th ANNIVERSARY
of his arrest.

### ANAMORPHOSIS

Anamorphosis is a drawing that has been distorted. In order to see what it really depicts, you have to shift angles, by tilting your head for instance.

At first glance, you'll only notice metallic bars, but when moving around a little, you'll see much more that!

### 30 FEET TALL

**HOWICK**
**SOUTH AFRICA**

**2012**
YEAR OF CONSTRUCTION

**ARTIST:**
**MARCO CIANFANELLI**

**1994-1999**
Nelson Mandela was South Africa's first black president.

## GREEN POINT STADIUM

SOCCER WORLD CUP 2010

### 64,000 SEATS
21 CRANES, 2,300 WORKERS TO BUILD IT
### 164 FEET TALL

**33**

**KAPSTADT**
**SOUTH AFRICA**

(2007-2010)
**3 YEARS**
OF CONSTRUCTION

**ARCHITECTS:**
**GMP, LOUIS KAROL, POINT**

## REUNIFICATION MONUMENT

### 2 SNAKES
are wrapped around a pillar, their heads fusing at the top. This symbolizes the

### REUNIFICATION
of the two Cameroons: French and British.

**35**

## SUPREME COURT

**34**

**ARCHITECT:**
**LENTIN ARCHITECTURE FIRM**

(1994-1996)
**2 YEARS**
OF CONSTRUCTION

**WINDHOEK**
NAMIBIA

**YAOUNDÉ**
**CAMEROON**

**ARCHITECT:**
**SALOMON**

**1970**
YEAR OF CONSTRUCTION

# ASIA AND OCEANIA

**52 COUNTRIES**

ANKARA (TURKEY)

PAPEETE (TAHITI)

## Asia

Asia is the largest and most populous continent. Its architecture is extremely diverse, with a multitude of styles that have been greatly influenced by various religions such as Hinduism, Buddhism and Islam, and by the different empires that saw the light of day in Asia. Its contemporary architecture continually breaks records.

**4,188** million inhabitants

**57%** OF THE WORLD'S POPULATION

**AREA: 18,970,000 MI²**

**DENSITY: 33 PEOPLE PER SQUARE MILE**

### AVERAGE TEMPERATURE

**5 °F** IN VERKHOYANSK (RUSSIA)

**82 °F** IN JAKARTA (INDONESIA)

THE HEYDAR ALIYEV CENTER

Russia
Kazakhstan
Tajikistan
Kyrgyzstan

Uzbekistan

Georgia
Armenia
Turkey
Azerbaijan

BAKU

THE REGISTAN OF SAMARKAND

ID KAH MOSQUE

Turkmenistan

KASHGAR

AZADI TOWER
TEHRAN

Iran

FAISAL MOSQUE

ISLAMABAD

Afghanistan

Pakistan

Nepal

DELHI

AGRA

ISPAHAN

ALLAHVERDI KHAN BRIDGE

LOTUS TEMPLE

India

TAJ MAHAL

MUMBAI

Arabian Sea

ANTILIA
MEENAKSHI AMMAN TEMPLE

MADURAI

Sri Lanka

Indian Ocean

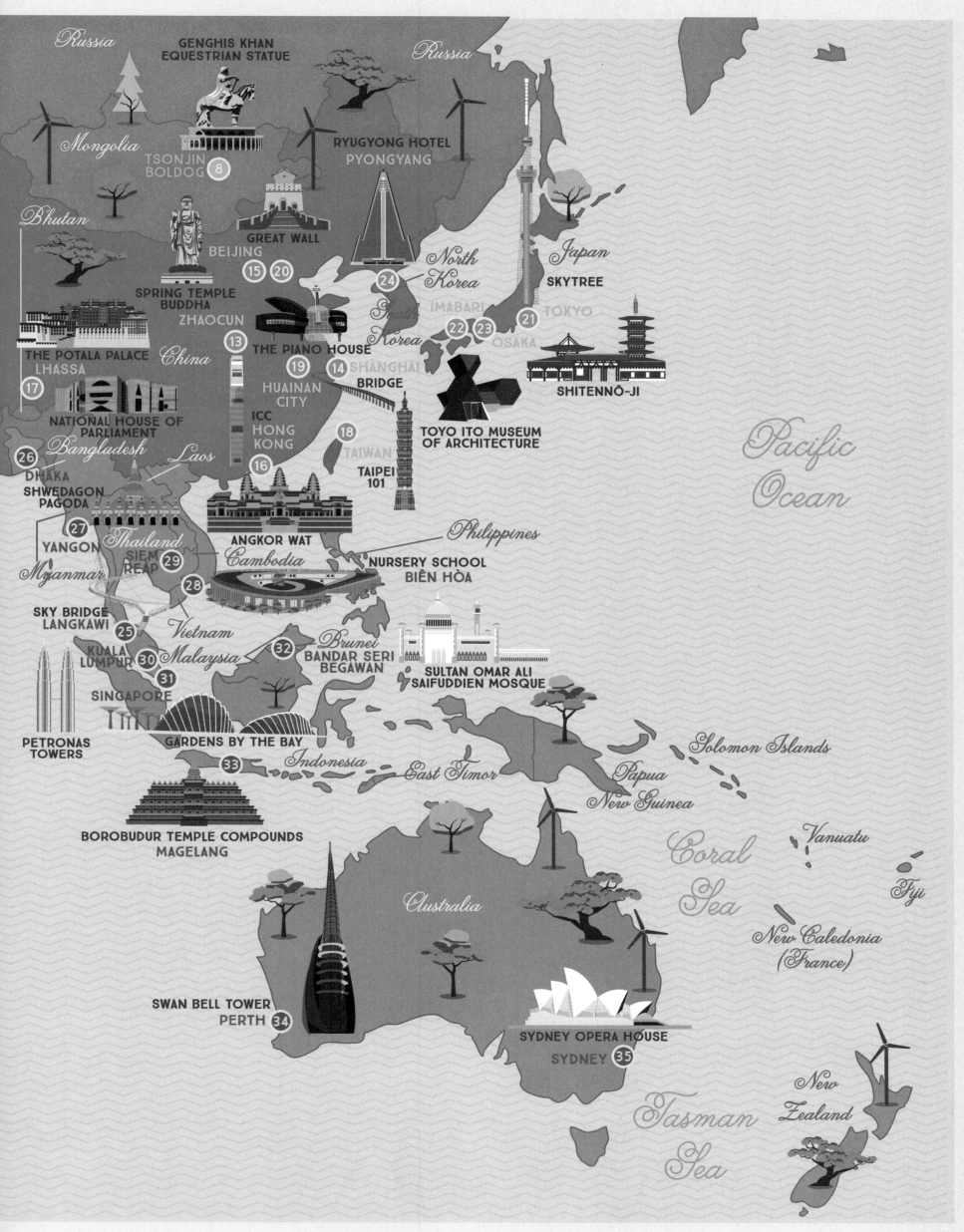

Russia

GENGHIS KHAN
EQUESTRIAN STATUE

Russia

Mongolia

TSONJIN
BOLDOG (8)

RYUGYONG HOTEL
PYONGYANG

Japan

SKYTREE

Bhutan

GREAT WALL

North
Korea

SPRING TEMPLE
BUDDHA

BEIJING

ZHAOCUN

(15) (20)

South
Korea

IMABARI

TOKYO

OSAKA

SKYTREE

THE PIANO HOUSE

(22) (23) (21)

SHITENNŌ-JI

(13)

THE POTALA PALACE
LHASSA

China

(19)

HUAINAN
CITY

SHANGHAI

(14)

BRIDGE

TOYO ITO MUSEUM
OF ARCHITECTURE

(17)

NATIONAL HOUSE OF
PARLIAMENT

Bangladesh

Laos

ICC
HONG
KONG

(18)

TAIWAN

Pacific
Ocean

(26)

DHAKA

(16)

TAIPEI
101

SHWEDAGON
PAGODA

(27)

YANGON

Thailand

SIEM
REAP

(29)

ANGKOR WAT

Cambodia

Philippines

Myanmar

(28)

NURSERY SCHOOL
BIÊN HÒA

SKY BRIDGE
LANGKAWI

(25)

Vietnam

Malaysia

Brunei
BANDAR SERI
BEGAWAN

KUALA
LUMPUR

(30)

(32)

(31)

SINGAPORE

SULTAN OMAR ALI
SAIFUDDIEN MOSQUE

PETRONAS
TOWERS

GARDENS BY THE BAY

Indonesia

East Timor

Papua
New Guinea

Solomon Islands

(33)

Vanuatu

BOROBUDUR TEMPLE COMPOUNDS
MAGELANG

Coral

Sea

Fiji

Australia

New Caledonia
(France)

SWAN BELL TOWER
PERTH (34)

SYDNEY OPERA HOUSE
SYDNEY (35)

New
Zealand

Tasman

Sea

# CENTRAL ASIA AND INDIAN PENINSULA

Map labels: AZERBAIJAN, MONGOLIA, UZBEKISTAN, IRAN, INDIA, PAKISTAN, Pacific Ocean, Indian Ocean

## TAJ MAHAL ①
means "the Crown of Palaces" in Persian.

### MAUSOLEUM FOR "THE LIGHT OF THE PALACE"
The Mughal emperor Shan Jahan commissioned this mausoleum in the memory of his wife Arjumand Banu Begam, nicknamed "the light of the palace", who died giving birth to her fourteenth child.

More than 1,000 elephants ensured the transportation of precious stones and marble used in the palace's construction. **1,000**

**ONE OF THE SEVEN WONDERS OF THE WORLD**

**UNESCO** World Heritage Site since 1983

**3 MILLION VISITORS PER YEAR**

**AGRA INDIA**

**(1631-1654) 23 YEARS OF CONSTRUCTION**

**ARCHITECT: USTAD AHMAD LAHAURI**

**STYLE: Mughal Architecture**

## ANTILIA ②
This house is **390,000 FT²** as large as 5 soccer fields, and houses a family of only six people!

**568 FT TALL**
**THE BIGGEST HOUSE IN THE WORLD**
**27 FLOORS**

**(2006-2010) 4 YEARS OF CONSTRUCTION**

**MUMBAI INDIA**

## QUTB MINAR
**235 FT TALL**
**379 STEPS**

**THE HIGHEST MINARET IN INDIA.**
**THE 3RD HIGHEST MINARET IN THE WORLD**

The adjacent Quwwat ul-Islam mosque was the first one to be built in India.

**(1192-1368) 176 YEARS OF CONSTRUCTION**

**DELHI INDIA** ③

## LOTUS TEMPLE
Bahai place of worship ④

**27 PETALS ON 9 SIDES**

**ARCHITECT: FARIBORZ SAHBA**

**(1980-1986) 6 YEARS OF CONSTRUCTION**

**NEW DELHI INDIA**

## MEENAKSHI AMMAN TEMPLE ⑤
The Meenakshi temple dates back to the 17th century. It houses 12 gateway towers known as **"GOPURAMS".**
These towers are also used as entrance doors. The temple is highly ornate, with **33,000 STATUES.**

**HINDU TEMPLE DEDICATED TO PARVATI, WIFE OF SHIVA**

**MADURAI INDIA**

**(1560-1660) 100 YEARS OF CONSTRUCTION**

## ALLAHVERDI KHAN BRIDGE ⑥

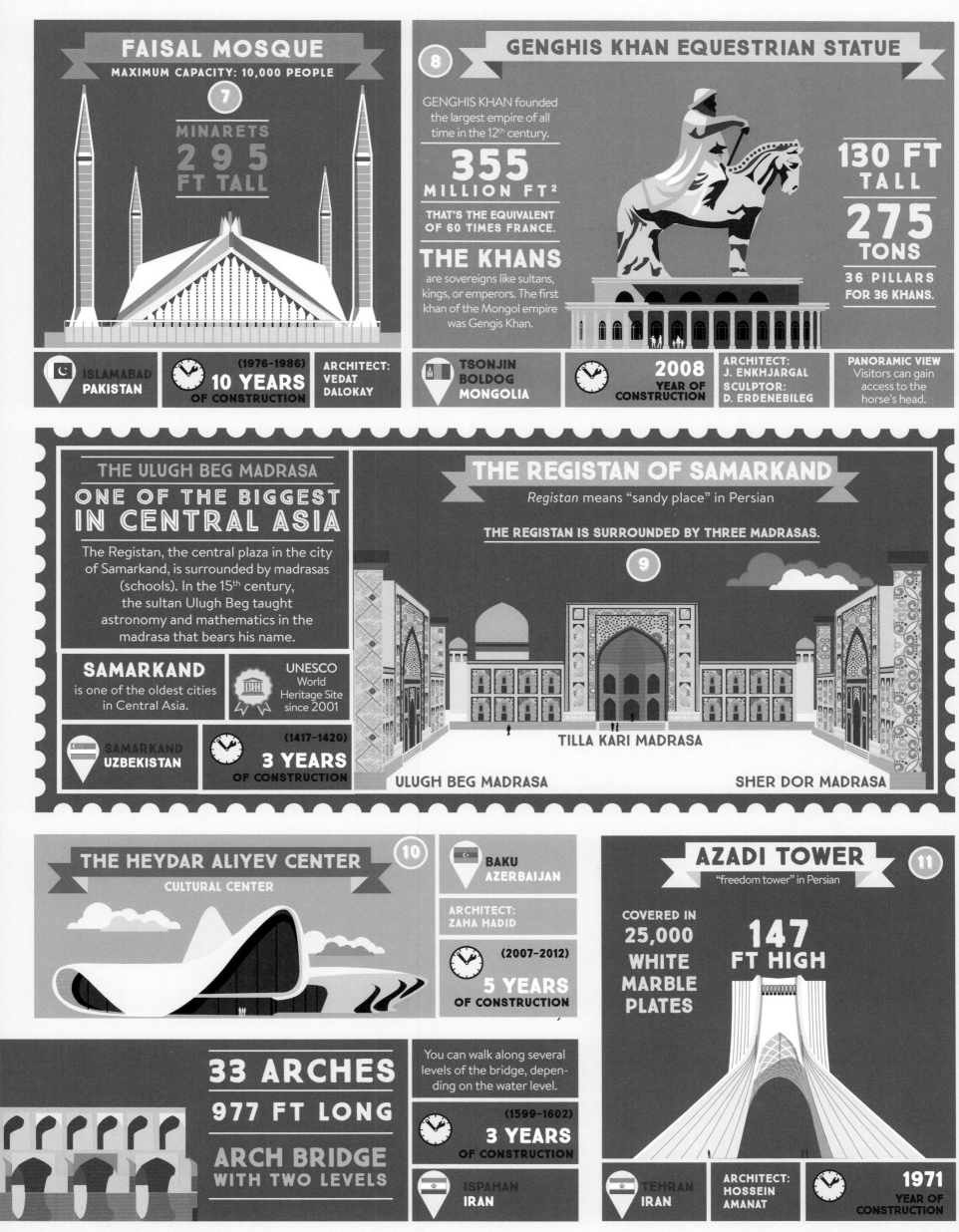

## FAISAL MOSQUE
**MAXIMUM CAPACITY: 10,000 PEOPLE**

7

**MINARETS**
**2 9 5**
**FT TALL**

ISLAMABAD
**PAKISTAN**

(1976–1986)
**10 YEARS**
OF CONSTRUCTION

ARCHITECT:
VEDAT DALOKAY

## GENGHIS KHAN EQUESTRIAN STATUE

8

GENGHIS KHAN founded the largest empire of all time in the 12th century.

**355**
MILLION FT²

**THAT'S THE EQUIVALENT OF 60 TIMES FRANCE.**

### THE KHANS
are sovereigns like sultans, kings, or emperors. The first khan of the Mongol empire was Gengis Khan.

**130 FT**
**TALL**

**275**
**TONS**

**36 PILLARS FOR 36 KHANS.**

TSONJIN BOLDOG
**MONGOLIA**

**2008**
YEAR OF CONSTRUCTION

ARCHITECT:
J. ENKHJARGAL
SCULPTOR:
D. ERDENEBILEG

**PANORAMIC VIEW**
Visitors can gain access to the horse's head.

---

### THE ULUGH BEG MADRASA
## ONE OF THE BIGGEST IN CENTRAL ASIA

The Registan, the central plaza in the city of Samarkand, is surrounded by madrasas (schools). In the 15th century, the sultan Ulugh Beg taught astronomy and mathematics in the madrasa that bears his name.

**SAMARKAND**
is one of the oldest cities in Central Asia.

UNESCO World Heritage Site since 2001

SAMARKAND
**UZBEKISTAN**

(1417–1420)
**3 YEARS**
OF CONSTRUCTION

## THE REGISTAN OF SAMARKAND
*Registan* means "sandy place" in Persian

**THE REGISTAN IS SURROUNDED BY THREE MADRASAS.**

9

**TILLA KARI MADRASA**

**ULUGH BEG MADRASA**

**SHER DOR MADRASA**

---

### THE HEYDAR ALIYEV CENTER
**CULTURAL CENTER**

10

BAKU
**AZERBAIJAN**

ARCHITECT:
ZAHA HADID

(2007–2012)
**5 YEARS**
OF CONSTRUCTION

## 33 ARCHES
**977 FT LONG**

**ARCH BRIDGE**
WITH TWO LEVELS

You can walk along several levels of the bridge, depending on the water level.

(1599–1602)
**3 YEARS**
OF CONSTRUCTION

ISPAHAN
**IRAN**

## AZADI TOWER
"freedom tower" in Persian

11

**COVERED IN 25,000 WHITE MARBLE PLATES**

**147**
**FT HIGH**

TEHRAN
**IRAN**

ARCHITECT:
HOSSEIN AMANAT

**1971**
YEAR OF CONSTRUCTION

## ASIA
## FAR EAST

NORTH KOREA

CHINA

JAPAN

Pacific Ocean

### ID KAH MOSQUE

With over **180,000 FT²**, (the equivalent of two soccer fields) the mosque can host up to 20,000 people.

**12**

**KASHGAR CHINA**

**1442** YEAR OF CONSTRUCTION

**THE BIGGEST MOSQUE IN CHINA**

### SPRING TEMPLE BUDDHA

**13**

### 420 FEET
### THE TALLEST STATUE IN THE WORLD

**2008** YEAR OF CONSTRUCTION

**ZHAOCUN CHINA**

### DANYANG-KUNSHAN GRAND BRIDGE

**102 MILES**

**14**

You would have to walk two days straight to go from the city of Danyang to Kunshan in Shanghai!

### THE LONGEST BRIDGE IN THE WORLD

(2008-2011) **3 YEARS** OF CONSTRUCTION

**JIANGSU CHINA**

### GREAT WALL

**ONE OF THE SEVEN WONDERS OF THE WORLD**

The Great Wall was built as a way to protect China's northern frontier.

### 12,425 MILES LONG

THE LONGEST CONSTRUCTION BY MAN **IN THE WORLD**

**1987**

**15**

**UNESCO WORLD HERITAGE SITE**

**SHANHAIGUAN - JIAYUGUAN CHINA**

(3ʳᵈ CENTURY B.C. - 17ᵀᴴ A.D.) **2,000 YEARS** OF CONSTRUCTION

### INTERNATIONAL COMMERCE CENTRE

**1,587** feet

**8ᵗʰ TALLEST** SKYSCRAPER in the world

**SKY 100** THE HIGHEST TERRACE in **HONG KONG**

**16**

ARCHITECT: **KOHN PEDERSEN FOX ASSOCIATES**

(2002-2010) **8 YEARS** OF CONSTRUCTION

**HONG KONG CHINA**

### THE POTALA PALACE
WHITE PALACE AND RED PALACE

**17**

#### THE DALAI LAMA'S WINTER PALACE

The Potala Palace extends over **1,400,000 FT².** That's the equivalent of **18 SOCCER** fields.

**LHASSA CHINA**

The Potala is built at **12,140 FT** ABOVE SEA LEVEL. The Red Palace is entirely dedicated to religious study and Buddhist prayers.

**17ᵀᴴ CENTURY** PERIOD OF CONSTRUCTION

The **WHITE PALACE** was built under the reign of the 5th dalai lama, Lozang Gyatso, and was the **TIBETAN GOVERNMENT'S HEADQUARTERS** as well as the **DALAI LAMAS' RESIDENCE** until 1959.

**UNESCO WORLD HERITAGE SITE** SINCE **1994**

### TAIPEI 101

**1,666** feet

**18**

**6ᵗʰ TALLEST** SKYSCRAPER in the world

**101** floors

**2004** EMPORIS SKYSCRAPER AWARD

ARCHITECT: **C.Y. LEE & PARTNERS ARCHITECTS**

(1999-2004) **5 YEARS** OF CONSTRUCTION

**TAIPEI, TAIWAN CHINA**

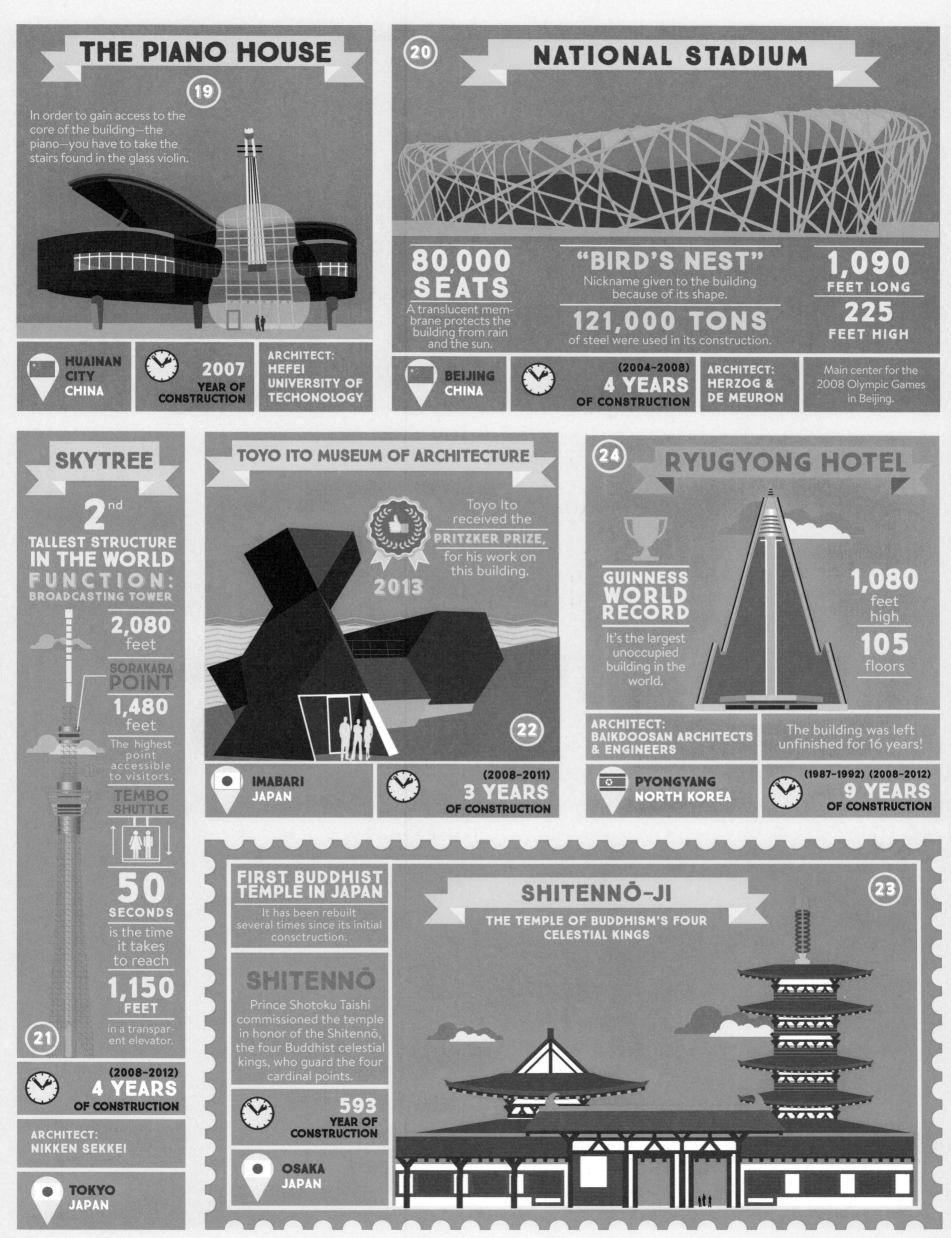

# THE PIANO HOUSE

(19)

In order to gain access to the core of the building—the piano—you have to take the stairs found in the glass violin.

HUAINAN CITY CHINA

2007 YEAR OF CONSTRUCTION

ARCHITECT: HEFEI UNIVERSITY OF TECHONOLOGY

## NATIONAL STADIUM

(20)

**80,000 SEATS**
A translucent membrane protects the building from rain and the sun.

**"BIRD'S NEST"**
Nickname given to the building because of its shape.

**121,000 TONS**
of steel were used in its construction.

**1,090 FEET LONG**

**225 FEET HIGH**

BEIJING CHINA

(2004-2008) **4 YEARS** OF CONSTRUCTION

ARCHITECT: HERZOG & DE MEURON

Main center for the 2008 Olympic Games in Beijing.

## SKYTREE

**2nd** TALLEST STRUCTURE IN THE WORLD
FUNCTION: BROADCASTING TOWER

**2,080** feet

SORAKARA POINT
**1,480** feet
The highest point accessible to visitors.

TEMBO SHUTTLE

**50 SECONDS**
is the time it takes to reach
**1,150 FEET**
in a transparent elevator.

(21)

(2008-2012) **4 YEARS** OF CONSTRUCTION

ARCHITECT: NIKKEN SEKKEI

TOKYO JAPAN

## TOYO ITO MUSEUM OF ARCHITECTURE

Toyo Ito received the **PRITZKER PRIZE**, for his work on this building.

2013

(22)

IMABARI JAPAN

(2008-2011) **3 YEARS** OF CONSTRUCTION

## RYUGYONG HOTEL

(24)

**GUINNESS WORLD RECORD**
It's the largest unoccupied building in the world.

**1,080** feet high

**105** floors

ARCHITECT: BAIKDOOSAN ARCHITECTS & ENGINEERS

The building was left unfinished for 16 years!

PYONGYANG NORTH KOREA

(1987-1992) (2008-2012) **9 YEARS** OF CONSTRUCTION

## SHITENNŌ-JI

**FIRST BUDDHIST TEMPLE IN JAPAN**
It has been rebuilt several times since its initial consctruction.

## SHITENNŌ

Prince Shotoku Taishi commissioned the temple in honor of the Shitennō, the four Buddhist celestial kings, who guard the four cardinal points.

**593** YEAR OF CONSTRUCTION

OSAKA JAPAN

THE TEMPLE OF BUDDHISM'S FOUR CELESTIAL KINGS

(23)

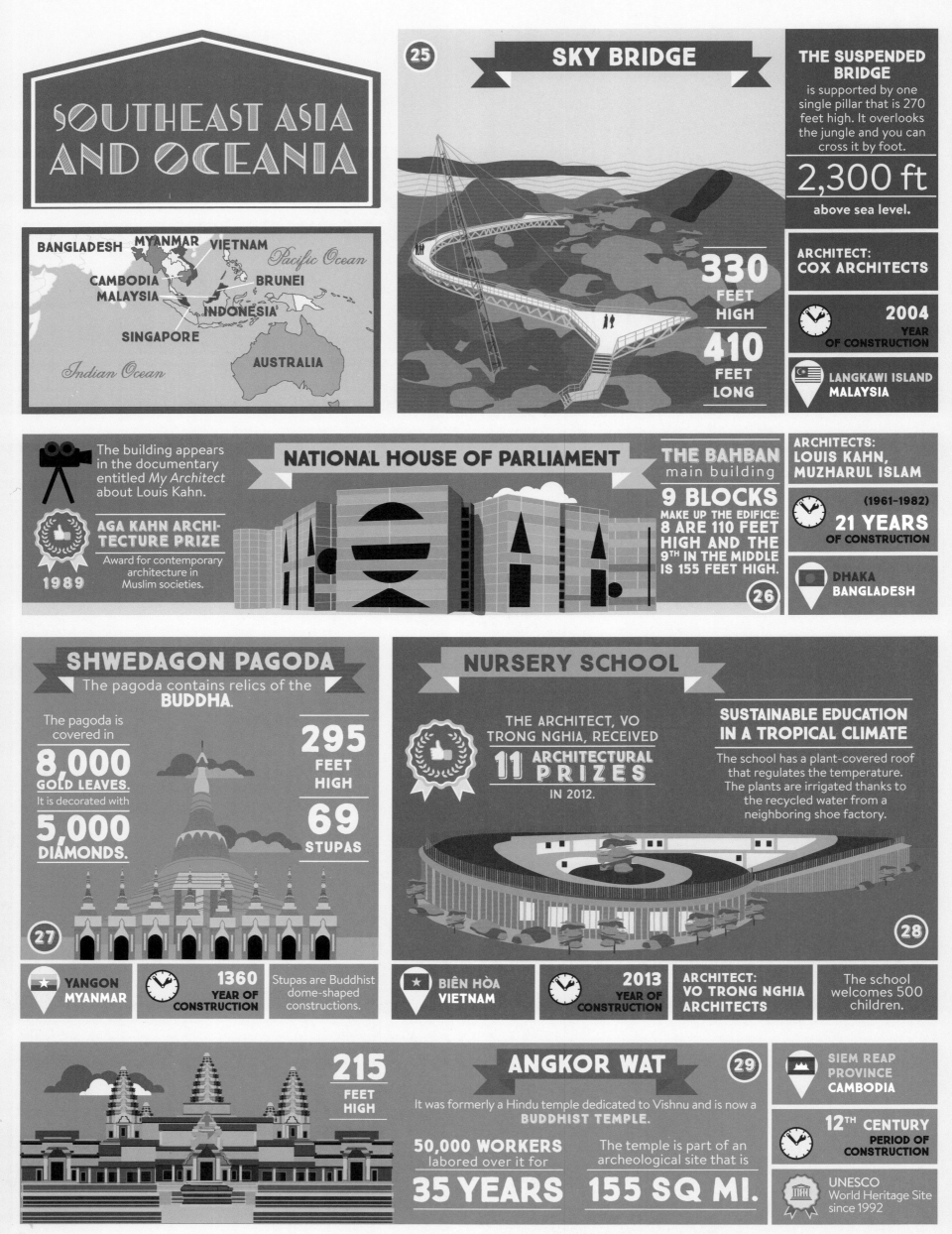

# SOUTHEAST ASIA AND OCEANIA

**BANGLADESH** · **MYANMAR** · **VIETNAM**
*Pacific Ocean*
**CAMBODIA** · **BRUNEI**
**MALAYSIA**
**INDONESIA**
**SINGAPORE**
*Indian Ocean* · **AUSTRALIA**

## 25 — SKY BRIDGE

**THE SUSPENDED BRIDGE** is supported by one single pillar that is 270 feet high. It overlooks the jungle and you can cross it by foot.

**2,300 ft** above sea level.

**330 FEET HIGH**

**410 FEET LONG**

**ARCHITECT: COX ARCHITECTS**

**2004** YEAR OF CONSTRUCTION

**LANGKAWI ISLAND MALAYSIA**

## NATIONAL HOUSE OF PARLIAMENT — 26

The building appears in the documentary entitled *My Architect* about Louis Kahn.

**AGA KAHN ARCHITECTURE PRIZE**
Award for contemporary architecture in Muslim societies.
**1989**

**THE BAHBAN** main building
**9 BLOCKS** MAKE UP THE EDIFICE: 8 ARE 110 FEET HIGH AND THE 9TH IN THE MIDDLE IS 155 FEET HIGH.

**ARCHITECTS: LOUIS KAHN, MUZHARUL ISLAM**

**(1961–1982) 21 YEARS** OF CONSTRUCTION

**DHAKA BANGLADESH**

## SHWEDAGON PAGODA — 27

The pagoda contains relics of the **BUDDHA.**

The pagoda is covered in **8,000 GOLD LEAVES.** It is decorated with **5,000 DIAMONDS.**

**295 FEET HIGH**

**69 STUPAS**

**YANGON MYANMAR**

**1360** YEAR OF CONSTRUCTION

Stupas are Buddhist dome-shaped constructions.

## NURSERY SCHOOL — 28

THE ARCHITECT, VO TRONG NGHIA, RECEIVED **11 ARCHITECTURAL PRIZES** IN 2012.

**SUSTAINABLE EDUCATION IN A TROPICAL CLIMATE**
The school has a plant-covered roof that regulates the temperature. The plants are irrigated thanks to the recycled water from a neighboring shoe factory.

**BIÊN HÒA VIETNAM**

**2013** YEAR OF CONSTRUCTION

**ARCHITECT: VO TRONG NGHIA ARCHITECTS**

The school welcomes 500 children.

## ANGKOR WAT — 29

**215 FEET HIGH**

It was formerly a Hindu temple dedicated to Vishnu and is now a **BUDDHIST TEMPLE.**

**50,000 WORKERS** labored over it for **35 YEARS**

The temple is part of an archeological site that is **155 SQ MI.**

**SIEM REAP PROVINCE CAMBODIA**

**12TH CENTURY** PERIOD OF CONSTRUCTION

UNESCO World Heritage Site since 1992

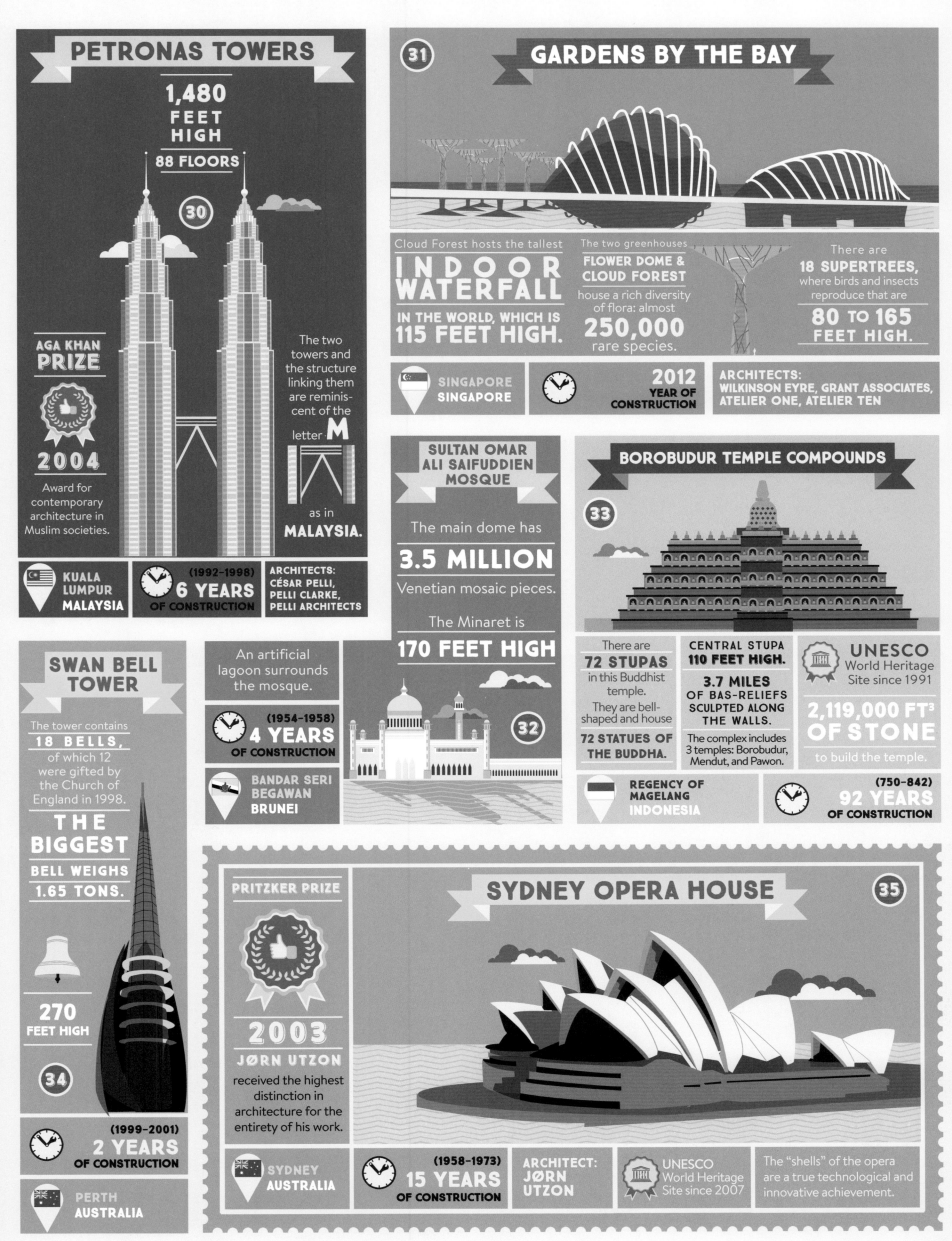

## PETRONAS TOWERS

**1,480 FEET HIGH**

**88 FLOORS**

30

**AGA KHAN PRIZE**

**2004**

Award for contemporary architecture in Muslim societies.

The two towers and the structure linking them are reminiscent of the letter **M** as in **MALAYSIA**.

| | | |
|---|---|---|
| **KUALA LUMPUR MALAYSIA** | **(1992-1998) 6 YEARS** OF CONSTRUCTION | **ARCHITECTS:** CÉSAR PELLI, PELLI CLARKE, PELLI ARCHITECTS |

## GARDENS BY THE BAY

31

Cloud Forest hosts the tallest **INDOOR WATERFALL** IN THE WORLD, WHICH IS **115 FEET HIGH.**

The two greenhouses **FLOWER DOME & CLOUD FOREST** house a rich diversity of flora: almost **250,000** rare species.

There are **18 SUPERTREES,** where birds and insects reproduce that are **80 TO 165 FEET HIGH.**

| | | |
|---|---|---|
| **SINGAPORE SINGAPORE** | **2012 YEAR OF CONSTRUCTION** | **ARCHITECTS:** WILKINSON EYRE, GRANT ASSOCIATES, ATELIER ONE, ATELIER TEN |

## SULTAN OMAR ALI SAIFUDDIEN MOSQUE

The main dome has **3.5 MILLION** Venetian mosaic pieces.

The Minaret is **170 FEET HIGH**

An artificial lagoon surrounds the mosque.

| | |
|---|---|
| **(1954-1958) 4 YEARS** OF CONSTRUCTION | |
| **BANDAR SERI BEGAWAN BRUNEI** | 32 |

## BOROBUDUR TEMPLE COMPOUNDS

33

There are **72 STUPAS** in this Buddhist temple. They are bell-shaped and house **72 STATUES OF THE BUDDHA.**

**CENTRAL STUPA 110 FEET HIGH.** **3.7 MILES OF BAS-RELIEFS SCULPTED ALONG THE WALLS.** The complex includes 3 temples: Borobudur, Mendut, and Pawon.

**UNESCO** World Heritage Site since 1991 **2,119,000 FT³ OF STONE** to build the temple.

| | |
|---|---|
| **REGENCY OF MAGELANG INDONESIA** | **(750-842) 92 YEARS** OF CONSTRUCTION |

## SWAN BELL TOWER

The tower contains **18 BELLS,** of which 12 were gifted by the Church of England in 1998.

**THE BIGGEST BELL WEIGHS 1.65 TONS.**

**270 FEET HIGH**

34

| |
|---|
| **(1999-2001) 2 YEARS** OF CONSTRUCTION |
| **PERTH AUSTRALIA** |

## SYDNEY OPERA HOUSE

35

**PRITZKER PRIZE**

**2003**

**JØRN UTZON**

received the highest distinction in architecture for the entirety of his work.

The "shells" of the opera are a true technological and innovative achievement.

| | | | |
|---|---|---|---|
| **SYDNEY AUSTRALIA** | **(1958-1973) 15 YEARS** OF CONSTRUCTION | **ARCHITECT: JØRN UTZON** | **UNESCO** World Heritage Site since 2007 |

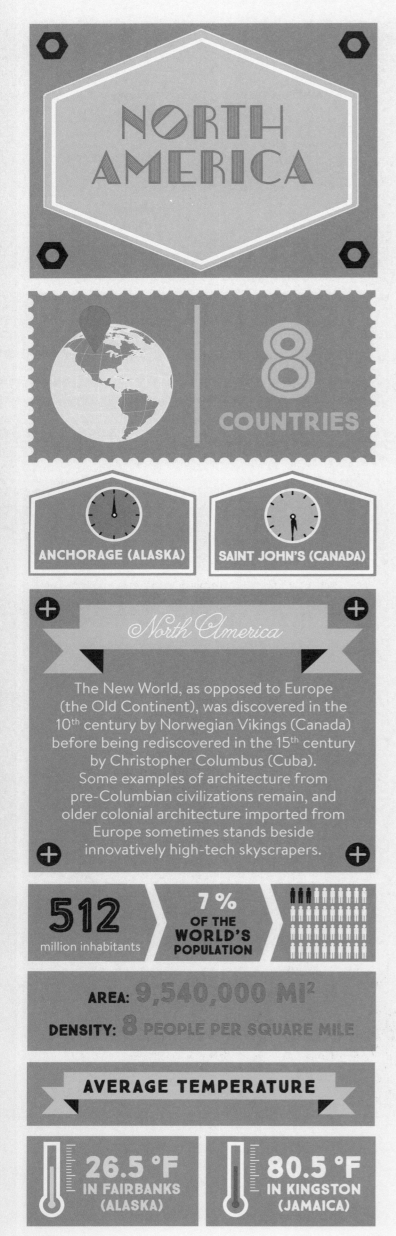

# NORTH AMERICA

**8 COUNTRIES**

ANCHORAGE (ALASKA)

SAINT JOHN'S (CANADA)

## North America

The New World, as opposed to Europe (the Old Continent), was discovered in the 10th century by Norwegian Vikings (Canada) before being rediscovered in the 15th century by Christopher Columbus (Cuba). Some examples of architecture from pre-Columbian civilizations remain, and older colonial architecture imported from Europe sometimes stands beside innovatively high-tech skyscrapers.

**512** million inhabitants

**7%** OF THE WORLD'S POPULATION

AREA: **9,540,000 MI²**

DENSITY: **8** PEOPLE PER SQUARE MILE

## AVERAGE TEMPERATURE

**26.5 °F** IN FAIRBANKS (ALASKA)

**80.5 °F** IN KINGSTON (JAMAICA)

ART GALLERY OF ALBERTA

EDMONTON ①

⑤ SCOTIABANK SADDLEDOME CALGARY

VANCOUVER ②

MUNICIPAL LIBRARY

SEATTLE ③

CENTRAL LIBRARY

GOLDEN GATE BRIDGE

④ SAN FRANCISCO

LAS VEGAS ⑥

CLEVELAND CLINIC

*Pacific Ocean*

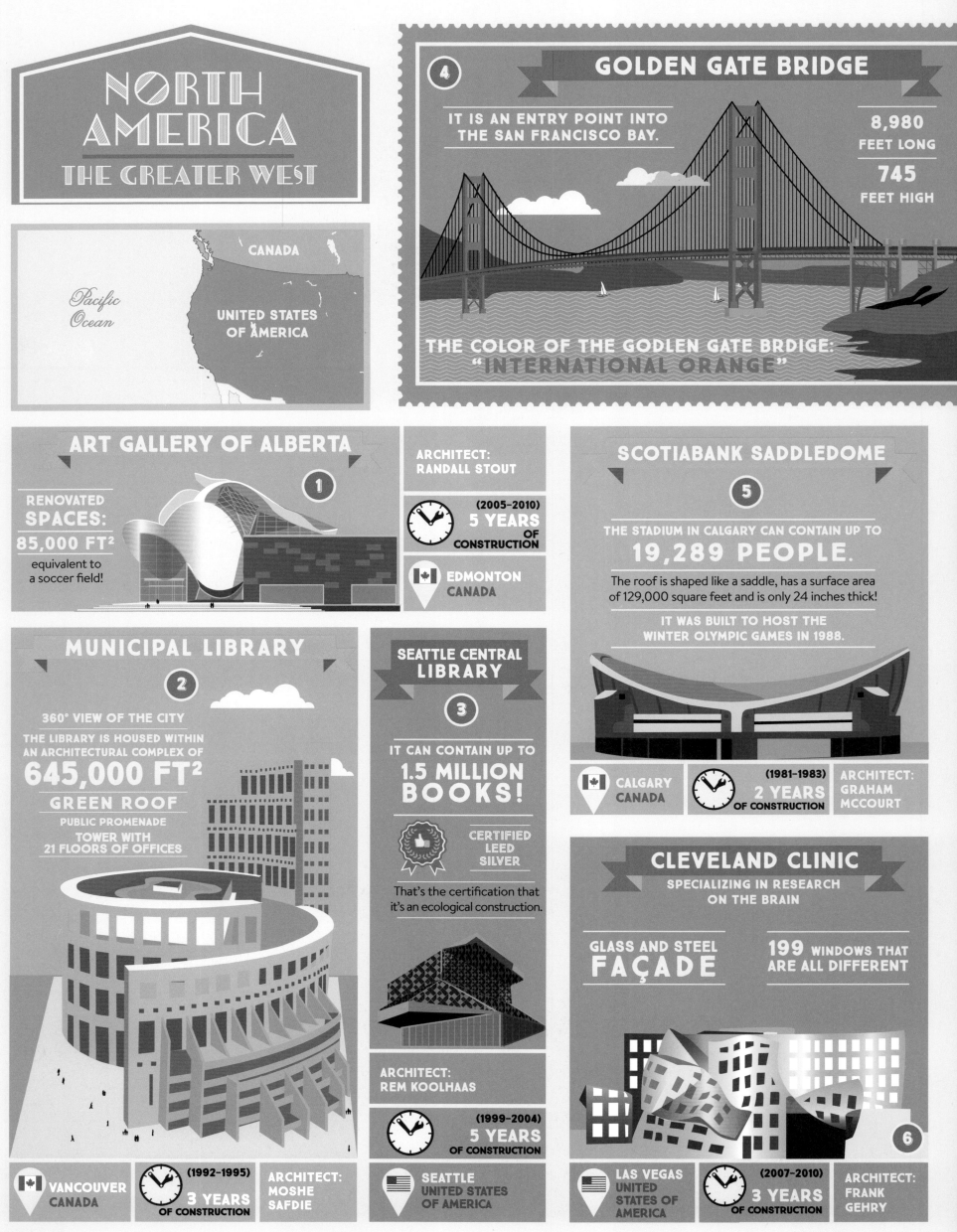

# NORTH AMERICA
## THE GREATER WEST

CANADA

Pacific Ocean

UNITED STATES OF AMERICA

### GOLDEN GATE BRIDGE

4

IT IS AN ENTRY POINT INTO THE SAN FRANCISCO BAY.

8,980 FEET LONG

745 FEET HIGH

THE COLOR OF THE GODLEN GATE BRDIGE: "INTERNATIONAL ORANGE"

### ART GALLERY OF ALBERTA

1

RENOVATED SPACES: 85,000 FT² equivalent to a soccer field!

ARCHITECT: RANDALL STOUT

(2005-2010) 5 YEARS OF CONSTRUCTION

EDMONTON CANADA

### MUNICIPAL LIBRARY

2

360° VIEW OF THE CITY

THE LIBRARY IS HOUSED WITHIN AN ARCHITECTURAL COMPLEX OF 645,000 FT²

GREEN ROOF

PUBLIC PROMENADE

TOWER WITH 21 FLOORS OF OFFICES

VANCOUVER CANADA

(1992-1995) 3 YEARS OF CONSTRUCTION

ARCHITECT: MOSHE SAFDIE

### SEATTLE CENTRAL LIBRARY

3

IT CAN CONTAIN UP TO 1.5 MILLION BOOKS!

CERTIFIED LEED SILVER

That's the certification that it's an ecological construction.

ARCHITECT: REM KOOLHAAS

(1999-2004) 5 YEARS OF CONSTRUCTION

SEATTLE UNITED STATES OF AMERICA

### SCOTIABANK SADDLEDOME

5

THE STADIUM IN CALGARY CAN CONTAIN UP TO 19,289 PEOPLE.

The roof is shaped like a saddle, has a surface area of 129,000 square feet and is only 24 inches thick!

IT WAS BUILT TO HOST THE WINTER OLYMPIC GAMES IN 1988.

CALGARY CANADA

(1981-1983) 2 YEARS OF CONSTRUCTION

ARCHITECT: GRAHAM MCCOURT

### CLEVELAND CLINIC

SPECIALIZING IN RESEARCH ON THE BRAIN

GLASS AND STEEL FAÇADE

199 WINDOWS THAT ARE ALL DIFFERENT

6

LAS VEGAS UNITED STATES OF AMERICA

(2007-2010) 3 YEARS OF CONSTRUCTION

ARCHITECT: FRANK GEHRY

The bridge appears in at least 70 films or television series.

**IT IS A SUSPENSION BRIDGE**

**ARCHITECT: IRVING MORROW**

**(1933-1937) 4 YEARS** OF CONSTRUCTION

**SAN FRANCISCO** UNITED STATES OF AMERICA

# ASPEN ART MUSEUM

## 32,290 FT² EXHIBITION SPACE

**2014 PRITZKER PRIZE** the highest distinction in the field of architecture

7

**ASPEN** UNITED STATES OF AMERICA

**(2012-2014) 2 YEARS** OF CONSTRUCTION

**ARCHITECT: SHIGERU BAN**

# CADET CHAPEL

Part of the United States Air Force Academy

**17 SPIRES OF 148 FEET EACH**
6,235 ft above sea level

**3 CHAPELS 3 RELIGIONS**
The chapels are independent and represent the Catholic, Jewish, and Protestant faiths.

10

**COLORADO SPRINGS** UNITED STATES OF AMERICA

**(1956-1962) 6 YEARS** OF CONSTRUCTION

**ARCHITECTS: SKIDMORE, OWINGS & MERRILL, NETSCH**

# MOUNT RUSHMORE

GEORGE WASHINGTON
THOMAS JEFFERSON
THEODORE ROOSEVELT
ABRAHAM LINCOLN

8

MONUMENTAL SCULPTURE CARVED INTO GRANITE that represents four presidents that have shaped U.S. history.

## 60 FEET HIGH
## 400 WORKERS
## 495,000 TONS
of rock were removed from the mountain.

**2 MILLION VISITORS PER YEAR**

Mount Rushmore appears in more than 20 films and TV shows.

**ARTISTS: GUTZON AND LINCOLN BORGLUM**

**BLACK HILLS** UNITED STATES OF AMERICA

**(1927-1941) 14 YEARS** OF CONSTRUCTION

9

# ACOMA PUEBLO

Acoma means "People of the White Rock".

## THE OLDEST CONTINUOUSLY INHABITED COMMUNITY IN NORTH AMERICA.

To gain access to the mesa you would have to climb up a steep staircase carved right into the stone, which discouraged any assailants.

**MESA 360 FEET HIGH**

More than **250 HOUSES** have been counted. 30 people live on the mesa permanently.

**ACOMA PUEBLO** UNITED STATES OF AMERICA

**12TH CENTURY** PERIOD OF CONSTRUCTION

A mesa is a land formation with steep walls and a flat top.

# MUSEUM OF MODERN ART

It is made using only concrete, glass, granite, aluminum and steel—like most of Tadao Andō's architectural works.

**TADAO ANDŌ RECEIVED THE PRITZKER PRIZE** the highest distinction in the field of architecture.
1995

**Y-SHAPED COMLUMNS THAT ARE 40 FT HIGH**
These are the museum's symbol.

11

## 3,000 WORKS EXHIBITED 54,000 FT² OF EXHIBITION SPACE

**FORT WORTH** UNITED STATES OF AMERICA

**2002** YEAR OF CONSTRUCTION

**ARCHITECT: TADAO ANDŌ**

# NORTH AMERICA
## THE NORTHEAST

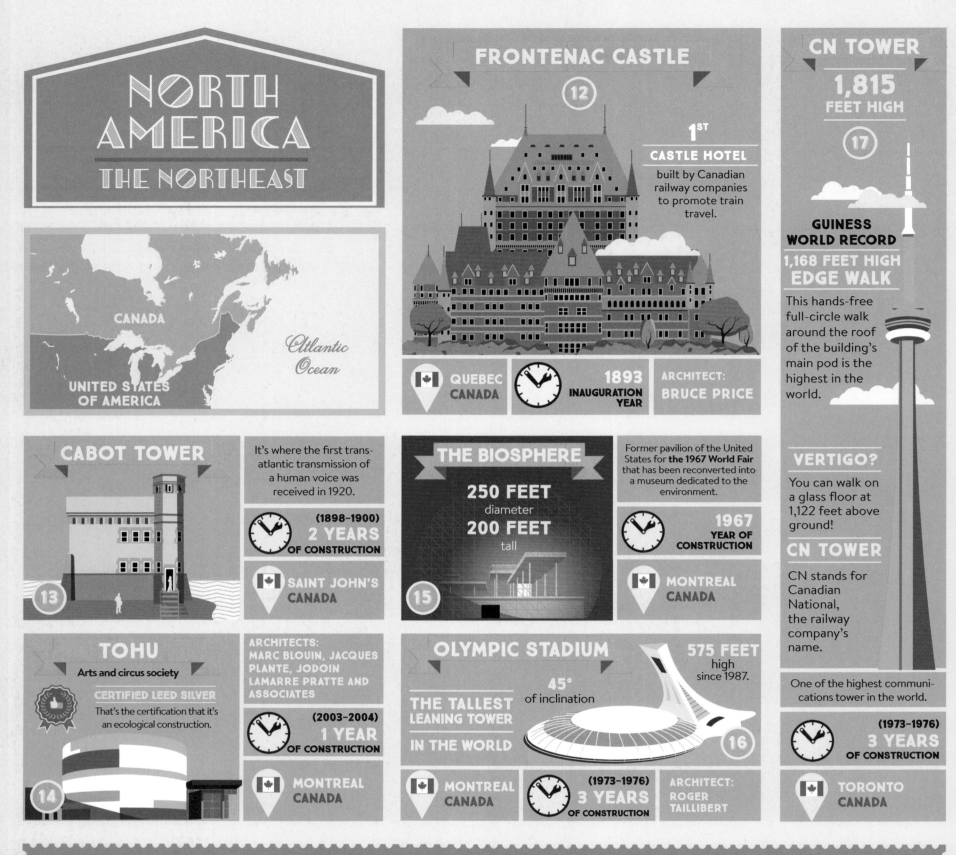

CANADA

UNITED STATES OF AMERICA

Atlantic Ocean

### FRONTENAC CASTLE
**12**

**1ST CASTLE HOTEL** built by Canadian railway companies to promote train travel.

QUEBEC CANADA

**1893** INAUGURATION YEAR

ARCHITECT: BRUCE PRICE

### CN TOWER
**1,815** FEET HIGH
**17**

**GUINESS WORLD RECORD**
**1,168 FEET HIGH EDGE WALK**

This hands-free full-circle walk around the roof of the building's main pod is the highest in the world.

**VERTIGO?**
You can walk on a glass floor at 1,122 feet above ground!

**CN TOWER**
CN stands for Canadian National, the railway company's name.

One of the highest communications tower in the world.

**(1973-1976) 3 YEARS** OF CONSTRUCTION

TORONTO CANADA

### CABOT TOWER
It's where the first trans-atlantic transmission of a human voice was received in 1920.

**(1898-1900) 2 YEARS** OF CONSTRUCTION

SAINT JOHN'S CANADA
**13**

### THE BIOSPHERE
**250 FEET** diameter
**200 FEET** tall
**15**

Former pavilion of the United States for **the 1967 World Fair** that has been reconverted into a museum dedicated to the environment.

**1967** YEAR OF CONSTRUCTION

MONTREAL CANADA

### TOHU
Arts and circus society

**CERTIFIED LEED SILVER**
That's the certification that it's an ecological construction.

ARCHITECTS: MARC BLOUIN, JACQUES PLANTE, JODOIN LAMARRE PRATTE AND ASSOCIATES

**(2003-2004) 1 YEAR** OF CONSTRUCTION

MONTREAL CANADA
**14**

### OLYMPIC STADIUM
**THE TALLEST LEANING TOWER IN THE WORLD**
**45°** of inclination
**575 FEET** high since 1987.

MONTREAL CANADA

**(1973-1976) 3 YEARS** OF CONSTRUCTION

ARCHITECT: ROGER TAILLIBERT
**16**

### THE CAPITOL
**18**

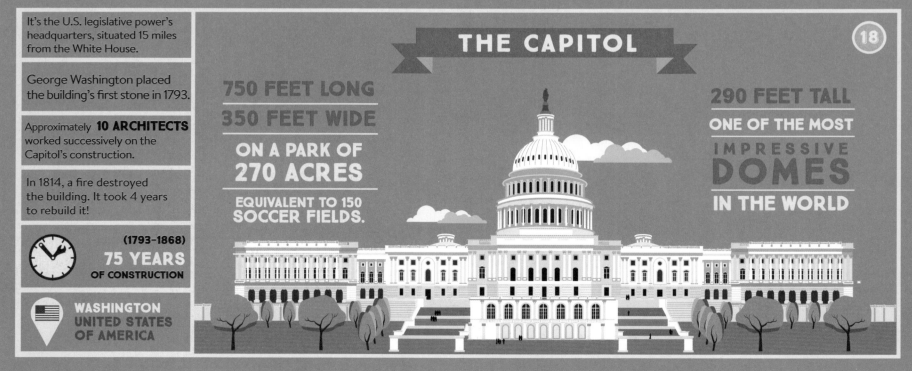

It's the U.S. legislative power's headquarters, situated 15 miles from the White House.

George Washington placed the building's first stone in 1793.

Approximately **10 ARCHITECTS** worked successively on the Capitol's construction.

In 1814, a fire destroyed the building. It took 4 years to rebuild it!

**(1793-1868) 75 YEARS** OF CONSTRUCTION

WASHINGTON UNITED STATES OF AMERICA

**750 FEET LONG**
**350 FEET WIDE**

**ON A PARK OF 270 ACRES**

**EQUIVALENT TO 150 SOCCER FIELDS.**

**290 FEET TALL**
**ONE OF THE MOST IMPRESSIVE DOMES IN THE WORLD**

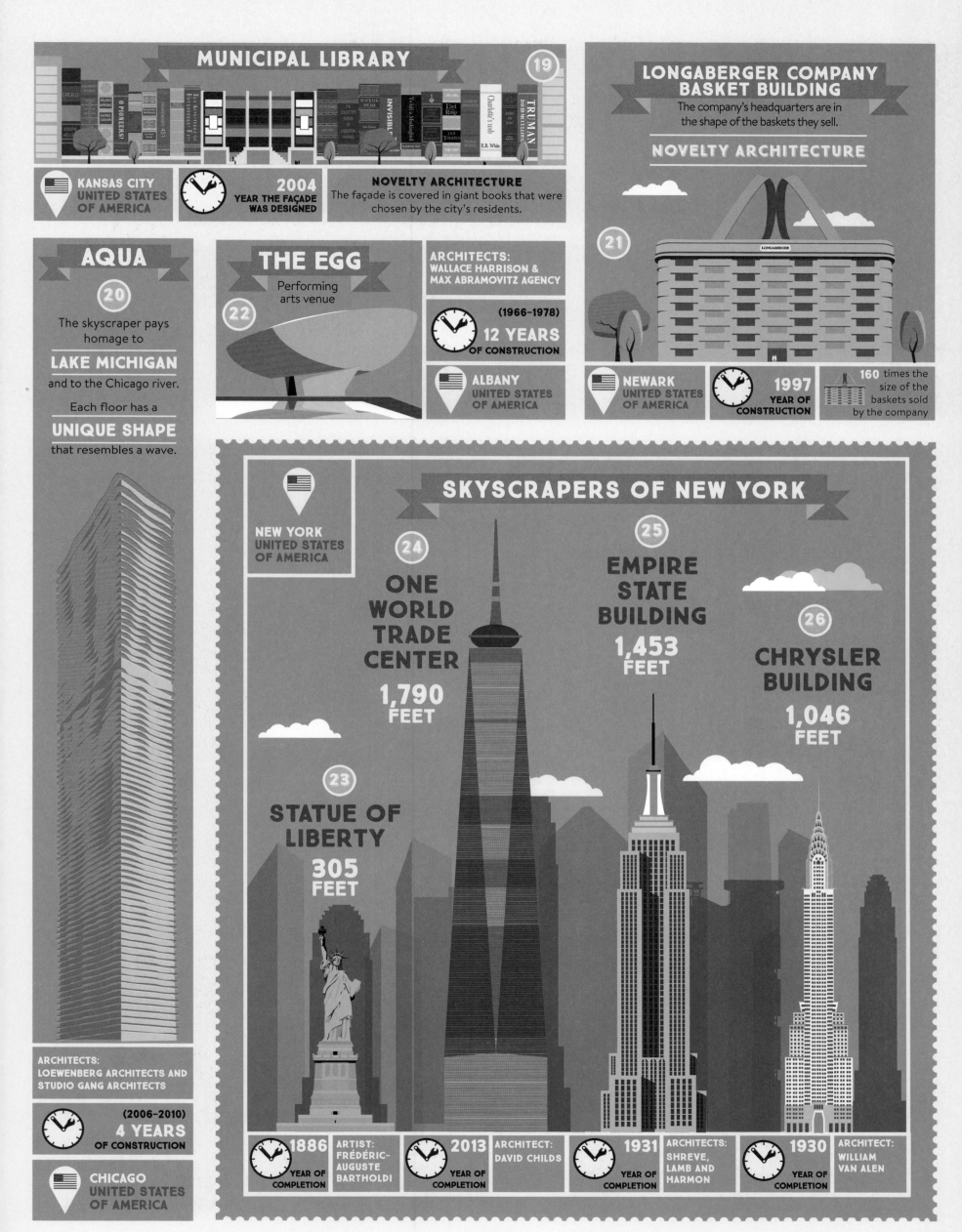

## MUNICIPAL LIBRARY

**19**

**KANSAS CITY UNITED STATES OF AMERICA**

**2004 YEAR THE FAÇADE WAS DESIGNED**

**NOVELTY ARCHITECTURE**
The façade is covered in giant books that were chosen by the city's residents.

## LONGABERGER COMPANY BASKET BUILDING
The company's headquarters are in the shape of the baskets they sell.

### NOVELTY ARCHITECTURE

**21**

**NEWARK UNITED STATES OF AMERICA**

**1997 YEAR OF CONSTRUCTION**

**160** times the size of the baskets sold by the company

## AQUA

**20**

The skyscraper pays homage to

**LAKE MICHIGAN**

and to the Chicago river.

Each floor has a

**UNIQUE SHAPE**

that resembles a wave.

**ARCHITECTS: LOEWENBERG ARCHITECTS AND STUDIO GANG ARCHITECTS**

**(2006–2010) 4 YEARS OF CONSTRUCTION**

**CHICAGO UNITED STATES OF AMERICA**

## THE EGG

Performing arts venue

**22**

**ARCHITECTS: WALLACE HARRISON & MAX ABRAMOVITZ AGENCY**

**(1966–1978) 12 YEARS OF CONSTRUCTION**

**ALBANY UNITED STATES OF AMERICA**

## SKYSCRAPERS OF NEW YORK

**NEW YORK UNITED STATES OF AMERICA**

**24 ONE WORLD TRADE CENTER 1,790 FEET**

**25 EMPIRE STATE BUILDING 1,453 FEET**

**26 CHRYSLER BUILDING 1,046 FEET**

**23 STATUE OF LIBERTY 305 FEET**

**1886 YEAR OF COMPLETION**

**ARTIST: FRÉDÉRIC-AUGUSTE BARTHOLDI**

**2013 YEAR OF COMPLETION**

**ARCHITECT: DAVID CHILDS**

**1931 YEAR OF COMPLETION**

**ARCHITECTS: SHREVE, LAMB AND HARMON**

**1930 YEAR OF COMPLETION**

**ARCHITECT: WILLIAM VAN ALEN**

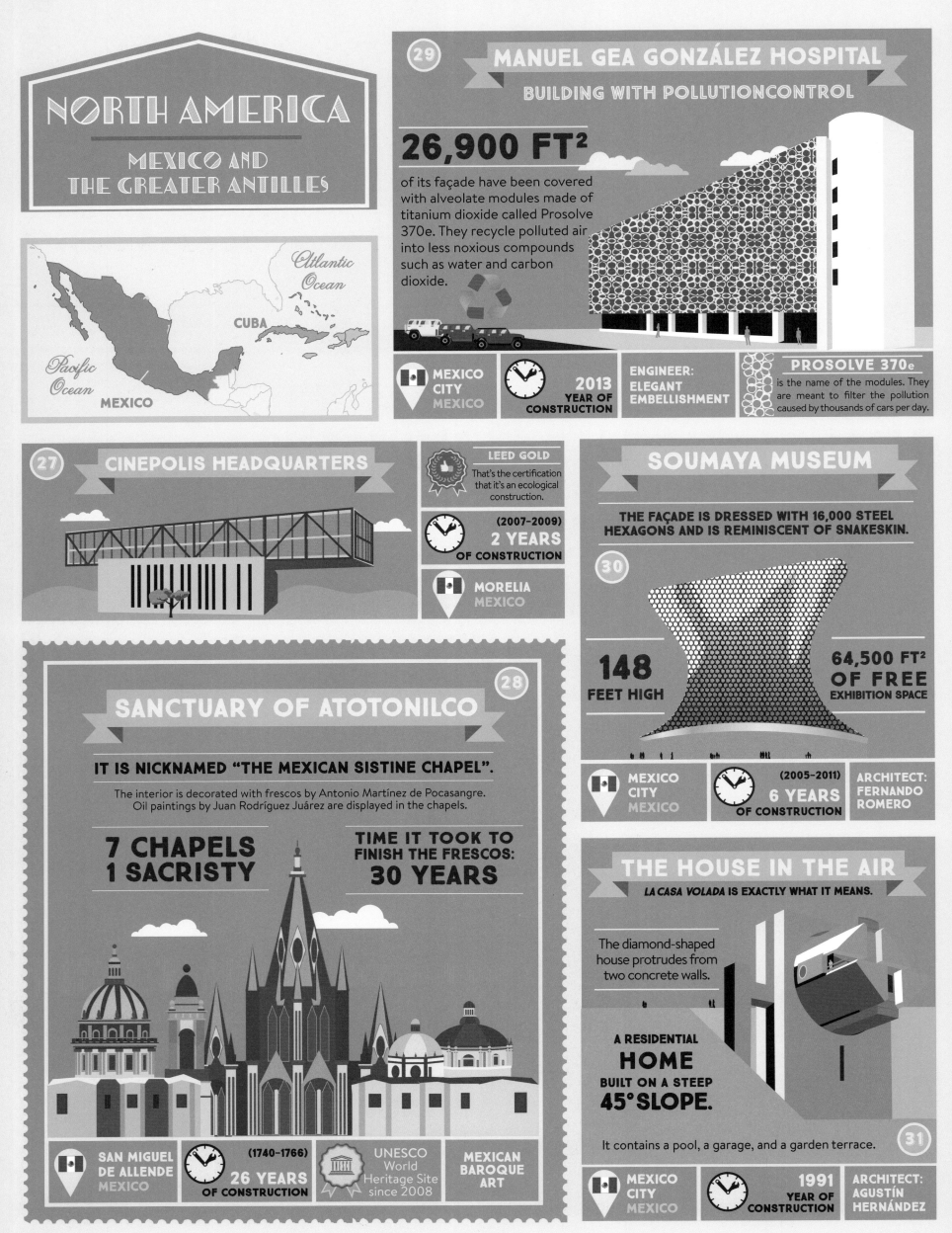

# NORTH AMERICA
## MEXICO AND THE GREATER ANTILLES

Atlantic Ocean

CUBA

Pacific Ocean

MEXICO

## (29) MANUEL GEA GONZÁLEZ HOSPITAL
### BUILDING WITH POLLUTIONCONTROL

**26,900 FT²**

of its façade have been covered with alveolate modules made of titanium dioxide called Prosolve 370e. They recycle polluted air into less noxious compounds such as water and carbon dioxide.

**MEXICO CITY** MEXICO

**2013** YEAR OF CONSTRUCTION

**ENGINEER: ELEGANT EMBELLISHMENT**

**PROSOLVE 370e** is the name of the modules. They are meant to filter the pollution caused by thousands of cars per day.

## (27) CINEPOLIS HEADQUARTERS

**LEED GOLD** That's the certification that it's an ecological construction.

**(2007–2009) 2 YEARS** OF CONSTRUCTION

**MORELIA** MEXICO

## SANCTUARY OF ATOTONILCO (28)

### IT IS NICKNAMED "THE MEXICAN SISTINE CHAPEL".

The interior is decorated with frescos by Antonio Martínez de Pocasangre. Oil paintings by Juan Rodríguez Juárez are displayed in the chapels.

**7 CHAPELS 1 SACRISTY**

**TIME IT TOOK TO FINISH THE FRESCOS: 30 YEARS**

**SAN MIGUEL DE ALLENDE** MEXICO

**(1740–1766) 26 YEARS** OF CONSTRUCTION

**UNESCO** World Heritage Site since 2008

**MEXICAN BAROQUE ART**

## SOUMAYA MUSEUM

### THE FAÇADE IS DRESSED WITH 16,000 STEEL HEXAGONS AND IS REMINISCENT OF SNAKESKIN.

(30)

**148 FEET HIGH**

**64,500 FT² OF FREE** EXHIBITION SPACE

**MEXICO CITY** MEXICO

**(2005–2011) 6 YEARS** OF CONSTRUCTION

**ARCHITECT: FERNANDO ROMERO**

## THE HOUSE IN THE AIR

*LA CASA VOLADA* IS EXACTLY WHAT IT MEANS.

The diamond-shaped house protrudes from two concrete walls.

**A RESIDENTIAL HOME BUILT ON A STEEP 45° SLOPE.**

It contains a pool, a garage, and a garden terrace.

(31)

**MEXICO CITY** MEXICO

**1991** YEAR OF CONSTRUCTION

**ARCHITECT: AGUSTÍN HERNÁNDEZ**

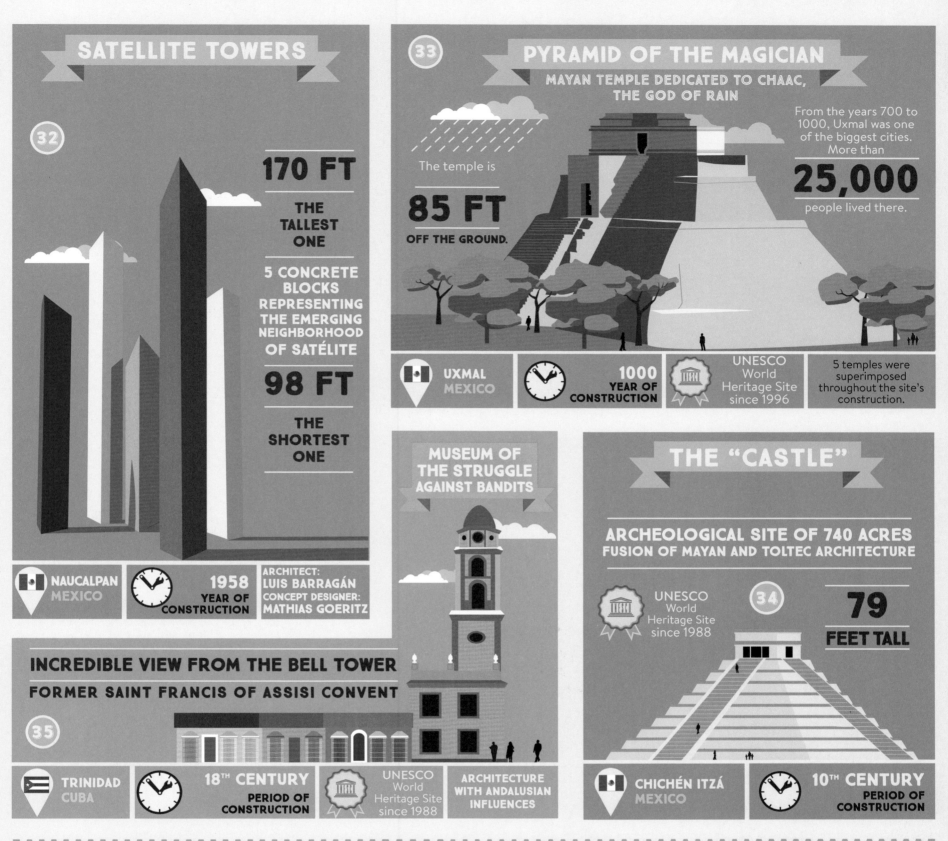

## SATELLITE TOWERS

(32)

**170 FT**
THE TALLEST ONE

**5 CONCRETE BLOCKS REPRESENTING THE EMERGING NEIGHBORHOOD OF SATÉLITE**

**98 FT**
THE SHORTEST ONE

NAUCALPAN MEXICO

**1958** YEAR OF CONSTRUCTION

ARCHITECT: LUIS BARRAGÁN
CONCEPT DESIGNER: MATHIAS GOERITZ

## (33) PYRAMID OF THE MAGICIAN
### MAYAN TEMPLE DEDICATED TO CHAAC, THE GOD OF RAIN

The temple is
**85 FT**
OFF THE GROUND.

From the years 700 to 1000, Uxmal was one of the biggest cities. More than
**25,000**
people lived there.

UXMAL MEXICO

**1000** YEAR OF CONSTRUCTION

UNESCO World Heritage Site since 1996

5 temples were superimposed throughout the site's construction.

## MUSEUM OF THE STRUGGLE AGAINST BANDITS

## INCREDIBLE VIEW FROM THE BELL TOWER
### FORMER SAINT FRANCIS OF ASSISI CONVENT

(35)

TRINIDAD CUBA

**18TH CENTURY** PERIOD OF CONSTRUCTION

UNESCO World Heritage Site since 1988

ARCHITECTURE WITH ANDALUSIAN INFLUENCES

## THE "CASTLE"

### ARCHEOLOGICAL SITE OF 740 ACRES
FUSION OF MAYAN AND TOLTEC ARCHITECTURE

UNESCO World Heritage Site since 1988

(34)

**79** FEET TALL

CHICHÉN ITZÁ MEXICO

**10TH CENTURY** PERIOD OF CONSTRUCTION

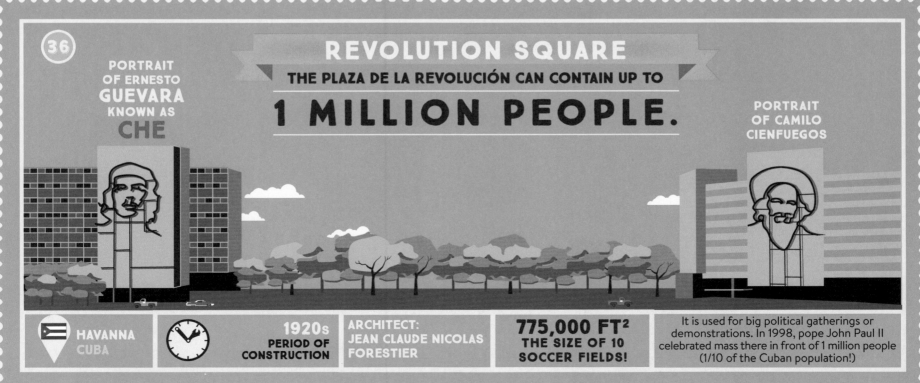

(36)

PORTRAIT OF ERNESTO **GUEVARA** KNOWN AS **CHE**

## REVOLUTION SQUARE
### THE PLAZA DE LA REVOLUCIÓN CAN CONTAIN UP TO
# 1 MILLION PEOPLE.

PORTRAIT OF CAMILO CIENFUEGOS

HAVANNA CUBA

**1920s** PERIOD OF CONSTRUCTION

ARCHITECT: JEAN CLAUDE NICOLAS FORESTIER

**775,000 FT²** THE SIZE OF 10 SOCCER FIELDS!

It is used for big political gatherings or demonstrations. In 1998, pope John Paul II celebrated mass there in front of 1 million people (1/10 of the Cuban population!)

TEMPLE I

Belize

Honduras

Venezuela

TIKAL ①

Guatemala

El Salvador

SAN FELIPE CASTLE

Nicaragua

Costa Rica

GRANADA ②

GRANADA CATHEDRAL

CARTAGENA

⑦

Colombia

⑧

TRUJILLO

Panama

③

PANAMA ④

⑤

VIRGIN OF PEACE

THE BIODIVERSITY MUSEUM

IPIALES

Ecuador

⑨

LAS LAJAS SANCTUARY

⑥

UNASUR HEADQUARTERS

QUITO

⑩

CUENCA

Peru

NEW CATHEDRAL

CHAN CHAN

TRUJILLO ㉔

⑤

LIMA ㉖

㉕

㉗ MACHU PICCHU

ARCHBISHOP'S PALACE

Bolivia

SUCRE ㉘

PALACE OF THE PREFECTURE

㉜ MOAI STATUES

EASTER ISLAND

(Chile)

NAVY BUILDING

VALPARAÍSO ㉛ ㉙

SANTIAGO ㉚

GRAN TORRE SANTIAGO

Pacific Ocean

Chile

CASTRO

㉝

CHURCH OF SAN FRANCISCO

Argentina

NAVE TIERRA ㉞

USHUAIA

MÉMORIAL ACTE
POINTE-À-PITRE
(12) Guadeloupe

Guyana
Suriname
(11) CAYENNE
UNIVERSITY LIBRARY
French Guiana

Brazil

NATAL
(15)

CATHEDRAL
OF BRASÍLIA

FORTRESS OF THE
THREE WISE MEN

BRASÍLIA (13)
(14)

COPAN
BUILDING

CHRIST THE
REDEEMER
RIO DE
JANEIRO

(17)
CONTEMPORARY ART MUSEUM
NITERÓI

(19)(20) (16)(18)
SÃO PAULO

Paraguay

(21) CURITIBA

OSCAR NIEMEYER MUSEUM

PALACIO
SALVO
Uruguay

MONTEVIDEO
(22)(23)
(35)(36)
PUNTA
BALLENA
BUENOS
AIRES
CASAPUEBLO

PUENTE DE LA MUJER

Atlantic
Ocean

CENTRAL
AND SOUTH
AMERICA

27

EASTER ISLAND (CHILE)        NATAL (BRAZIL)

South America

In Central and South America, two types
of architecture stand out: pre-Columbian style
(before Christopher Columbus' arrival),
which includes constructions made of clay
like those of the Incas, Mayas, and Aztecs;
colonial style, imported primarily by the
Spanish from the 16th century onwards, which can
be recognized by its elaborate details.
Contemporary architecture certainly doesn't
lag behind, with striking places such as
the city of Brasilia.

455
million inhabitants

6.2 %
OF THE
WORLD'S
POPULATION

SURFACE AREA: 7,085,000 MI²

DENSITY: 10 PEOPLE PER SQUARE MILE

AVERAGE TEMPERATURE

42.8 °F
IN USHUAIA
(ARGENTINA)

80.6 °F
IN MANAUS
(BRAZIL)

# CENTRAL AMERICA AND THE NORTH OF SOUTH AMERICA

GUATEMALA · NICARAGUA · GUADELOUPE · PANAMA · VENEZUELA · FRENCH GUIANA · COLOMBIA · ECUADOR

## THE BIODIVERSITY MUSEUM

3

The colorful architecture of the museum symbolizes Panama's narrow strip of land.

This isthmus joined North and South America **13 MILLION YEARS AGO.**

**43,000 FT²** OF EXHIBITION SPACE

ARCHITECT: FRANK GEHRY

(2004-2014) **10 YEARS** OF CONSTRUCTION

PANAMA CITY **PANAMA**

## TEMPLE I

Ah Cacao, one of the great Mayan sovereigns, is buried in this temple.

**154** FEET TALL

APPROX. **734** YEAR OF CONSTRUCTION

TIKAL NATIONAL PARK **GUATEMALA**

1

## GRANADA CATHEDRAL

2

The first cathedral dates back to 1583, but it was completely destroyed along with a part of the city in 1856 by William Walker (a mercenary from the U.S.) and his troupes. The cathedral's reconstruction was completed in 1915.

GRANADA **NICARAGUA**

**1915** YEAR OF CONSTRUCTION

ARCHITECT: ANDRÉS ZAPPATA

## PANAMA CANAL

4

**85 FT** ABOVE SEA LEVEL

**12 LOCKS**

**50 MI** LONG

**14,000 SHIPS**

**330 MILLION TONS** OF GOODS PER YEAR

AFTER 1914 **5,590 MI**

Panama Canal

**13,670 MI** BEFORE 1914

Cape Horn

PANAMA CITY **PANAMA**

(1881-1914) **33 YEARS** OF CONSTRUCTION

ENGINEER: GEORGE WASHINGTON GOETHALS

## TRUMP OCEAN CLUB HOTEL & TOWER

5

**930 FT TALL**

**70 FLOORS**

**37 ELEVATORS**

**47 SUITES**

**ONE CASINO**

A BEACH ON A PRIVATE ISLAND

ARCHITECT: ARIAS SERNA SARAVIA

**2011** YEAR OF INAUGURATION

PANAMA CITY **PANAMA**

## UNASUR HEADQUARTERS

6

**180 FT** OF CANTILEVERS

**UNASUR** is the Union of South American Nations.

ARCHITECT: DIEGO GUAYASAMÍN

(2012-2014) **2 YEARS** OF CONSTRUCTION

QUITO **ECUADOR**

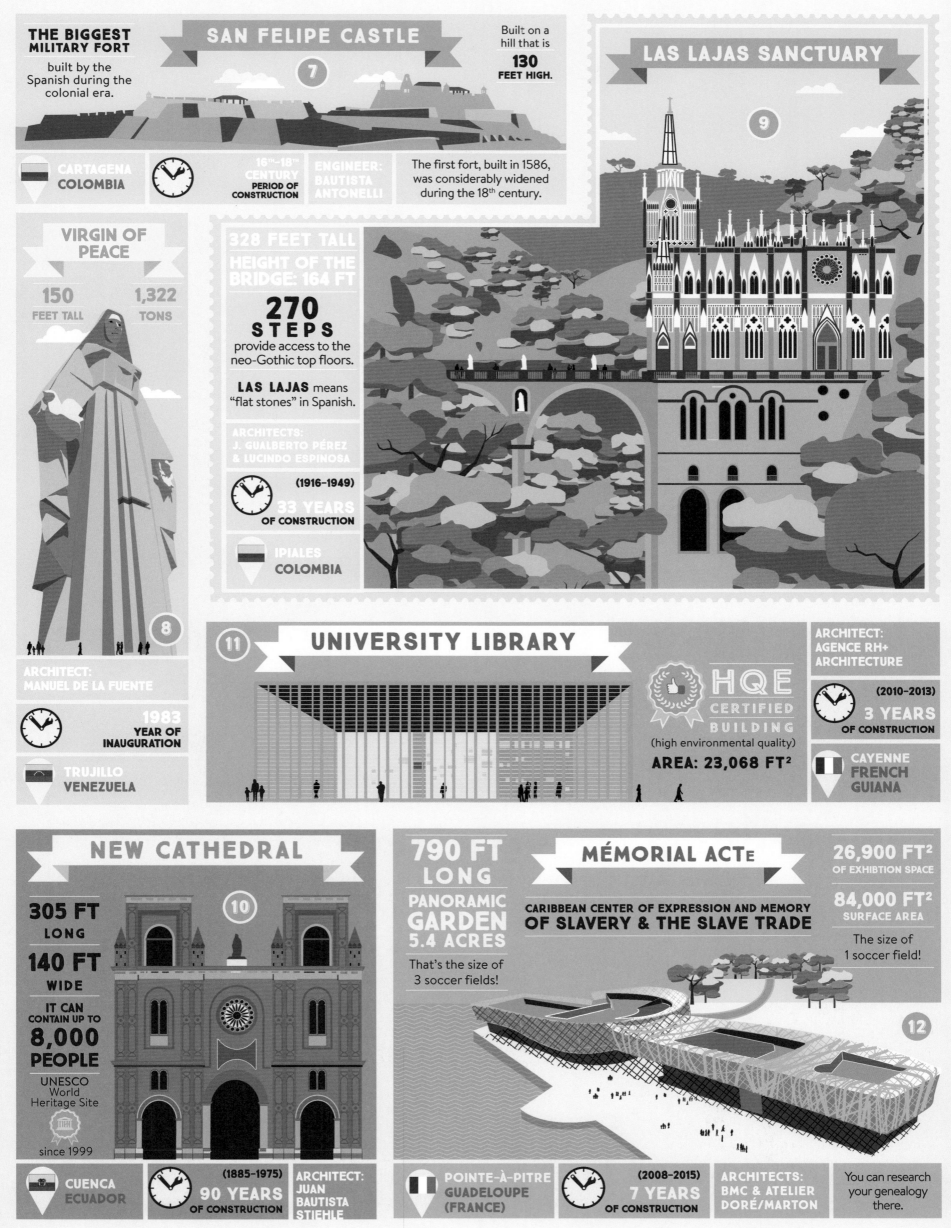

## THE BIGGEST MILITARY FORT

built by the Spanish during the colonial era.

### SAN FELIPE CASTLE

**7**

Built on a hill that is **130 FEET HIGH.**

**CARTAGENA COLOMBIA**

**16TH–18TH CENTURY** PERIOD OF CONSTRUCTION

**ENGINEER: BAUTISTA ANTONELLI**

The first fort, built in 1586, was considerably widened during the 18th century.

### LAS LAJAS SANCTUARY

**9**

### VIRGIN OF PEACE

**150** FEET TALL

**1,322** TONS

**ARCHITECT: MANUEL DE LA FUENTE**

**1983** YEAR OF INAUGURATION

**TRUJILLO VENEZUELA**

**8**

**328 FEET TALL** HEIGHT OF THE BRIDGE: 164 FT

**270 STEPS**

provide access to the neo-Gothic top floors.

**LAS LAJAS** means "flat stones" in Spanish.

**ARCHITECTS: J. GUALBERTO PÉREZ & LUCINDO ESPINOSA**

**(1916–1949)**

**33 YEARS** OF CONSTRUCTION

**IPIALES COLOMBIA**

### UNIVERSITY LIBRARY

**11**

**HQE CERTIFIED BUILDING**
(high environmental quality)
**AREA: 23,068 FT²**

**ARCHITECT: AGENCE RH+ ARCHITECTURE**

**(2010–2013)**

**3 YEARS** OF CONSTRUCTION

**CAYENNE FRENCH GUIANA**

### NEW CATHEDRAL

**10**

**305 FT** LONG

**140 FT** WIDE

IT CAN CONTAIN UP TO **8,000 PEOPLE**

UNESCO World Heritage Site

since 1999

**CUENCA ECUADOR**

**(1885–1975)**

**90 YEARS** OF CONSTRUCTION

**ARCHITECT: JUAN BAUTISTA STIEHLE**

**790 FT LONG**

PANORAMIC **GARDEN 5.4 ACRES**

That's the size of 3 soccer fields!

### MÉMORIAL ACTe

CARIBBEAN CENTER OF EXPRESSION AND MEMORY **OF SLAVERY & THE SLAVE TRADE**

**26,900 FT²** OF EXHIBITION SPACE

**84,000 FT²** SURFACE AREA

The size of 1 soccer field!

**12**

**POINTE-À-PITRE GUADELOUPE (FRANCE)**

**(2008–2015)**

**7 YEARS** OF CONSTRUCTION

**ARCHITECTS: BMC & ATELIER DORÉ/MARTON**

You can research your genealogy there.

# SOUTH AMERICA
## BRAZIL AND URUGUAY

**BRAZIL**

*Pacific Ocean*

*Atlantic Ocean*

**URUGUAY**

## FORTRESS OF THE THREE WISE MEN

15

The Fortress of the Three Wise Men was built by the Portuguese, who occupied Brazil from 1501. It predates the city of Natal's foundation, which took place on Christmas Day 1599.

The Dutch took over the fortress in 1633, but in 1654 the Portuguese took a hold of it again.

**NATAL BRAZIL**

**1598** YEAR OF CONSTRUCTION

## COPACABANA PALACE

16

**ARCHITECT: JOSEPH GIRE**

**130,000 FT²**
**222 ROOMS**

Many famous people such as Einstein and Walt Disney have stayed there.

**1923** YEAR OF INAUGURATION

**RIO DE JANEIRO BRAZIL**

## CATHEDRAL OF BRASÍLIA
### Metropolitan Cathedral of Our Lady of Aparecida

**130 FEET TALL**

**230** feet in diameter

13

THE STRUCTURE IS COMPOSED OF **16 CONCRETE COLUMNS** POINTING TO THE SKY. EACH ONE WEIGHS **99 TONS.**

**BRASÍLIA BRAZIL**

**(1958–1970) 12 YEARS OF CONSTRUCTION**

**ARCHITECT: OSCAR NIEMEYER**

**UNESCO World Heritage Site** — Since 1987

## BRAZILIAN NATIONAL CONGRESS

**ADMINISTRATIVE SERVICES**

IN 1988 **OSCAR NIEMEYER RECEIVED THE PRITZKER PRIZE** the highest distinction in the field of architecture

**SENATE**

**HOUSE OF REPRESENTATIVES**

14

The city of Brasília, which saw its first construction boom between 1956 and 1960, replaced Rio de Janeiro as Brazil's capital. Juscelino Kubitschek wanted to create a modern city and balance the distribution of the country's population, which tended to be concentrated along the coast.

**BRASÍLIA BRAZIL**

**1960** YEAR OF INAUGURATION

**ARCHITECT: OSCAR NIEMEYER**

Lucio Costa, the urbanist, conceived Brasília's design in the shape of a plane.

## CHRIST THE REDEEMER

**1,322 TONS**
Approximately the weight of 8 blue whales!

**125 FT TALL**

**2,310** FEET ABOVE SEA LEVEL ON MOUNT CORCOVADO

17

The statue was built in France in Landowski's sculpture studio before being shipped to Brazil by boat in separate parts. Christ's head alone came in 50 parts!

**RIO DE JANEIRO BRAZIL**

**1931** YEAR OF INAUGURATION

**SCULPTOR: PAUL LANDOWSKI**

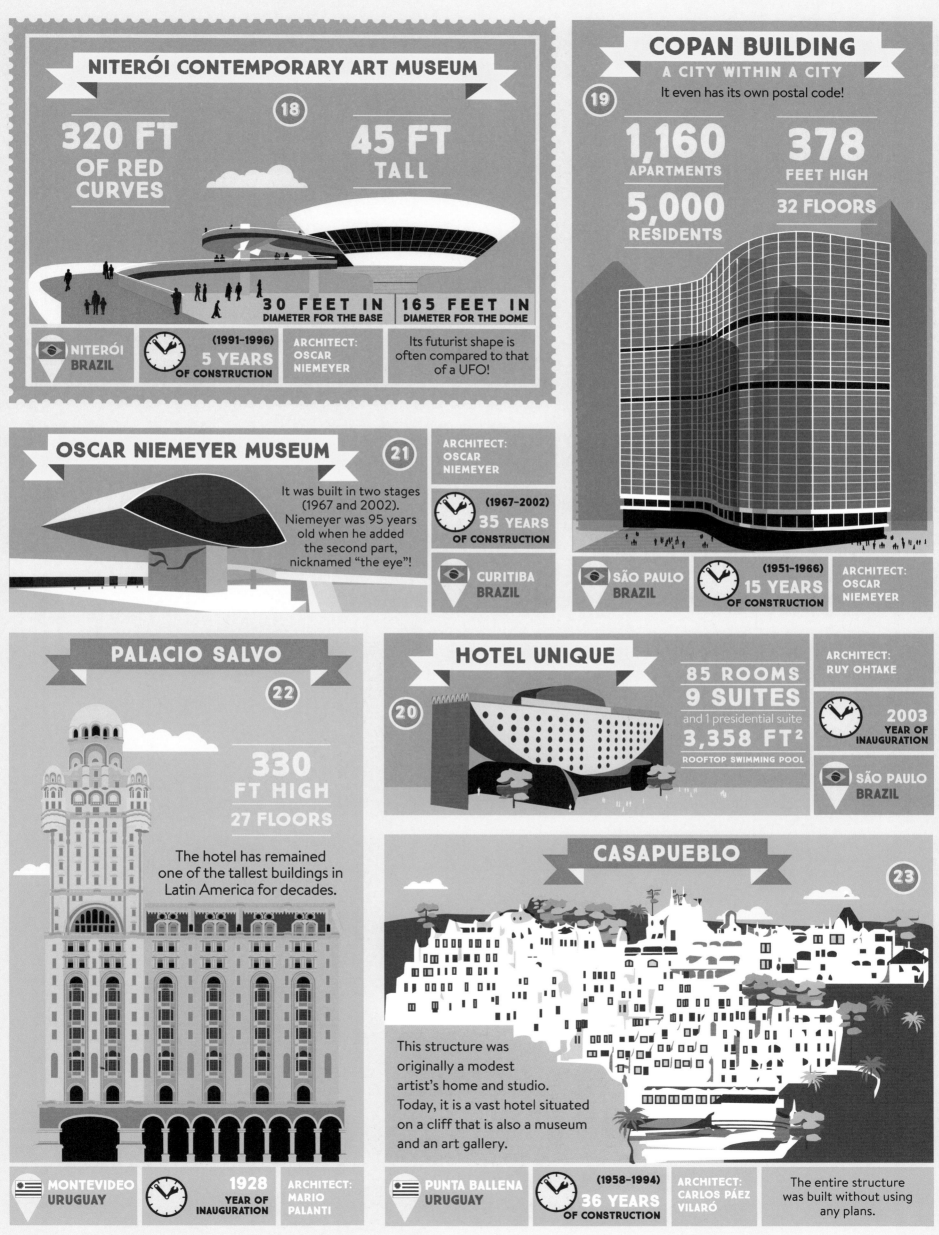

## NITERÓI CONTEMPORARY ART MUSEUM

**18**

**320 FT** OF RED CURVES

**45 FT** TALL

**30 FEET IN** DIAMETER FOR THE BASE

**165 FEET IN** DIAMETER FOR THE DOME

NITERÓI BRAZIL

**(1991-1996)** **5 YEARS** OF CONSTRUCTION

ARCHITECT: OSCAR NIEMEYER

Its futurist shape is often compared to that of a UFO!

## COPAN BUILDING

A CITY WITHIN A CITY

It even has its own postal code!

**19**

**1,160** APARTMENTS

**378** FEET HIGH

**5,000** RESIDENTS

**32 FLOORS**

SÃO PAULO BRAZIL

**(1951-1966)** **15 YEARS** OF CONSTRUCTION

ARCHITECT: OSCAR NIEMEYER

## OSCAR NIEMEYER MUSEUM

**21**

It was built in two stages (1967 and 2002). Niemeyer was 95 years old when he added the second part, nicknamed "the eye"!

ARCHITECT: OSCAR NIEMEYER

**(1967-2002)** **35 YEARS** OF CONSTRUCTION

CURITIBA BRAZIL

## PALACIO SALVO

**22**

**330 FT HIGH**

**27 FLOORS**

The hotel has remained one of the tallest buildings in Latin America for decades.

MONTEVIDEO URUGUAY

**1928** YEAR OF INAUGURATION

ARCHITECT: MARIO PALANTI

## HOTEL UNIQUE

**20**

ARCHITECT: RUY OHTAKE

**85 ROOMS** **9 SUITES** and 1 presidential suite

**3,358 FT²** ROOFTOP SWIMMING POOL

**2003** YEAR OF INAUGURATION

SÃO PAULO BRAZIL

## CASAPUEBLO

**23**

This structure was originally a modest artist's home and studio. Today, it is a vast hotel situated on a cliff that is also a museum and an art gallery.

PUNTA BALLENA URUGUAY

**(1958-1994)** **36 YEARS** OF CONSTRUCTION

ARCHITECT: CARLOS PÁEZ VILARÓ

The entire structure was built without using any plans.

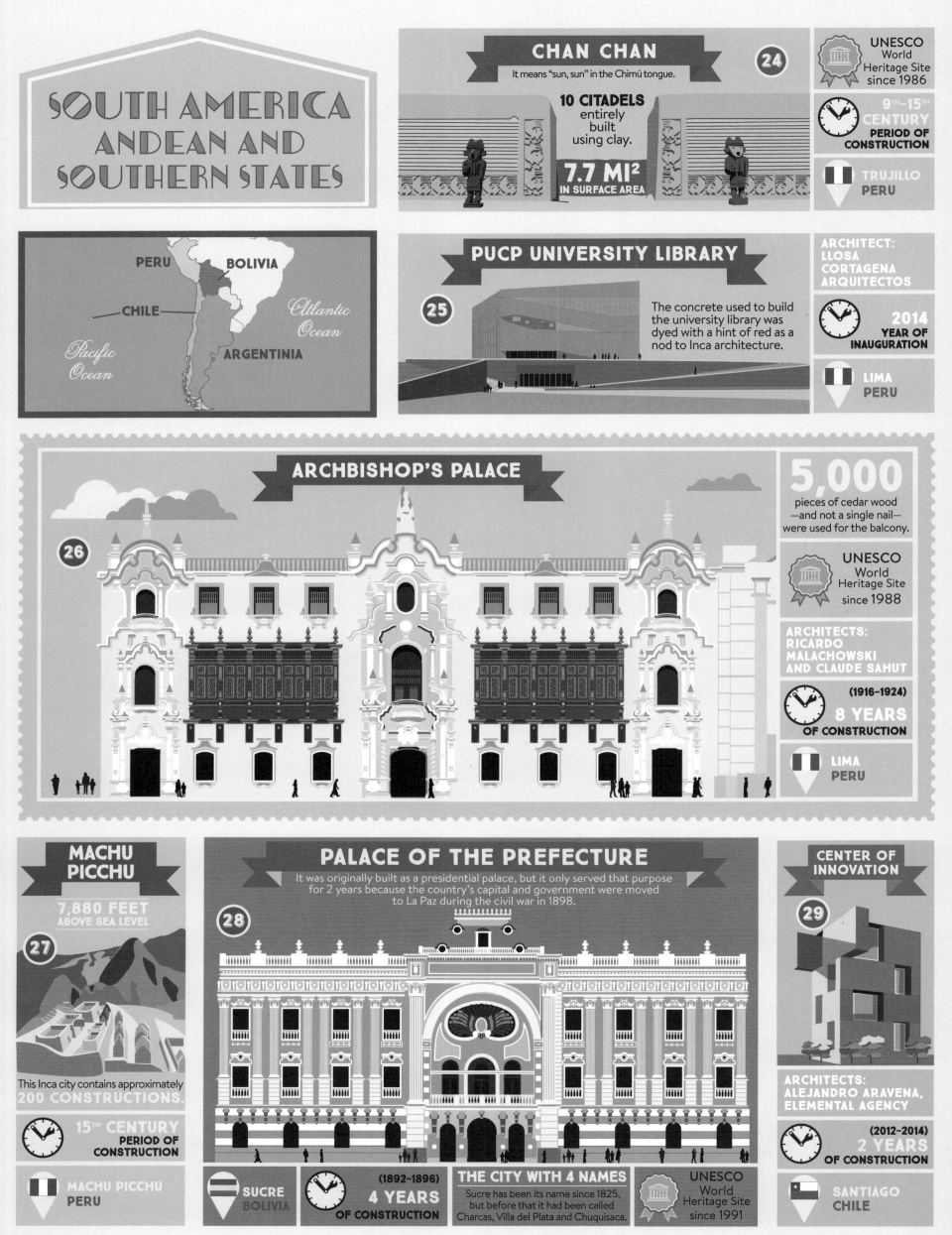

# SOUTH AMERICA ANDEAN AND SOUTHERN STATES

PERU
BOLIVIA
CHILE
Atlantic Ocean
Pacific Ocean
ARGENTINIA

## CHAN CHAN

It means "sun, sun" in the Chimú tongue.

**10 CITADELS** entirely built using clay.

**7.7 MI²** IN SURFACE AREA

24

UNESCO World Heritage Site since 1986

**9TH–15TH CENTURY** PERIOD OF CONSTRUCTION

TRUJILLO PERU

## PUCP UNIVERSITY LIBRARY

25

The concrete used to build the university library was dyed with a hint of red as a nod to Inca architecture.

ARCHITECT: LLOSA CORTAGENA ARQUITECTOS

**2014** YEAR OF INAUGURATION

LIMA PERU

## ARCHBISHOP'S PALACE

26

**5,000** pieces of cedar wood —and not a single nail— were used for the balcony.

UNESCO World Heritage Site since 1988

ARCHITECTS: RICARDO MALACHOWSKI AND CLAUDE SAHUT

**(1916–1924) 8 YEARS** OF CONSTRUCTION

LIMA PERU

## MACHU PICCHU

**7,880 FEET** ABOVE SEA LEVEL

27

This Inca city contains approximately **200 CONSTRUCTIONS.**

**15TH CENTURY** PERIOD OF CONSTRUCTION

MACHU PICCHU PERU

## PALACE OF THE PREFECTURE

It was originally built as a presidential palace, but it only served that purpose for 2 years because the country's capital and government were moved to La Paz during the civil war in 1898.

28

SUCRE BOLIVIA

**(1892–1896) 4 YEARS** OF CONSTRUCTION

### THE CITY WITH 4 NAMES

Sucre has been its name since 1825, but before that it had been called Charcas, Villa del Plata and Chuquisaca.

UNESCO World Heritage Site since 1991

## CENTER OF INNOVATION

29

ARCHITECTS: ALEJANDRO ARAVENA, ELEMENTAL AGENCY

**(2012–2014) 2 YEARS** OF CONSTRUCTION

SANTIAGO CHILE

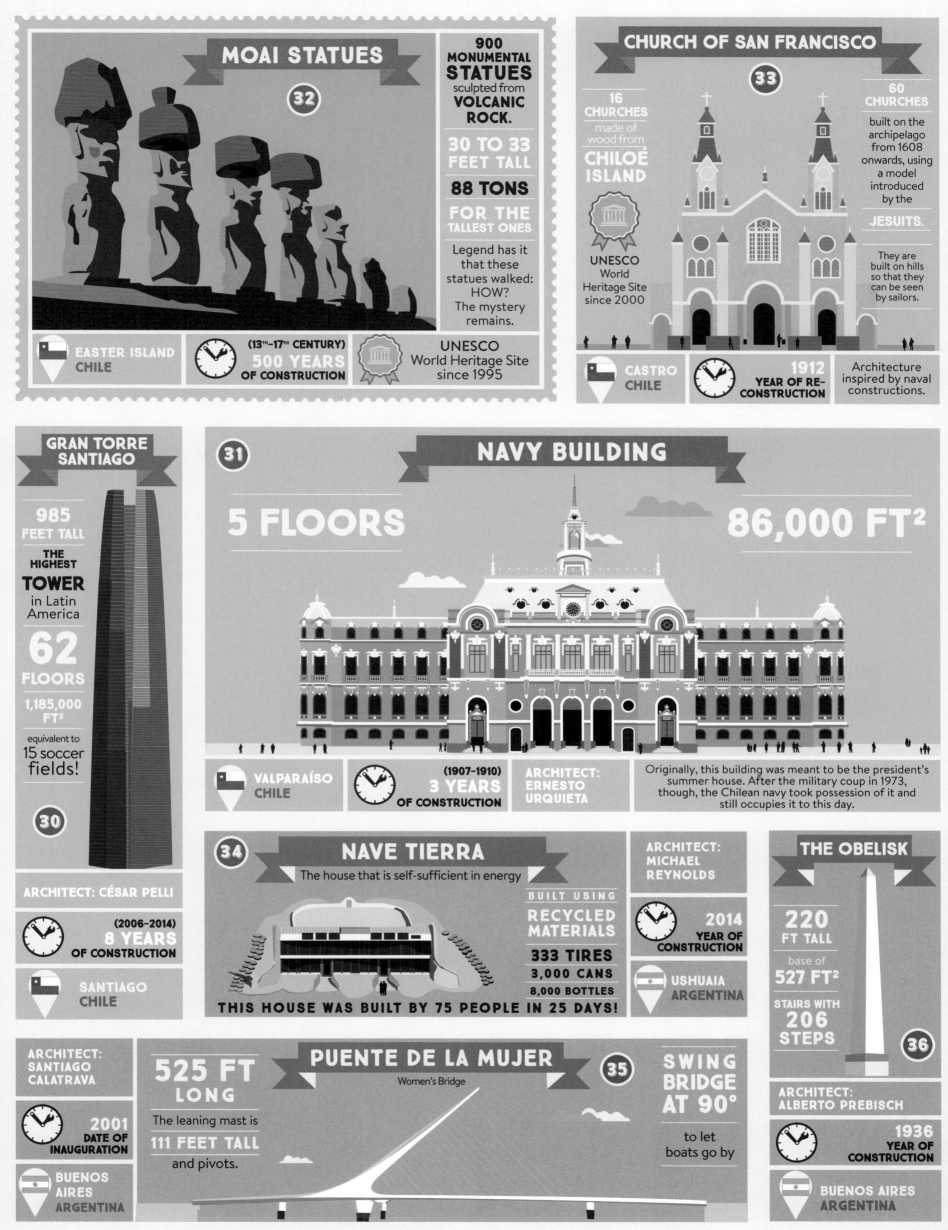

## MOAI STATUES

32

900 MONUMENTAL **STATUES** sculpted from **VOLCANIC ROCK.**

**30 TO 33 FEET TALL**

**88 TONS** FOR THE **TALLEST ONES**

Legend has it that these statues walked: HOW? The mystery remains.

**EASTER ISLAND CHILE**

(13TH–17TH CENTURY) **500 YEARS** OF CONSTRUCTION

UNESCO World Heritage Site since 1995

## CHURCH OF SAN FRANCISCO

33

**16 CHURCHES** made of wood from **CHILOÉ ISLAND**

UNESCO World Heritage Site since 2000

**60 CHURCHES** built on the archipelago from 1608 onwards, using a model introduced by the **JESUITS.**

They are built on hills so that they can be seen by sailors.

**CASTRO CHILE**

1912 YEAR OF RE-CONSTRUCTION

Architecture inspired by naval constructions.

## GRAN TORRE SANTIAGO

**985 FEET TALL**

THE HIGHEST **TOWER** in Latin America

**62 FLOORS**

1,185,000 FT² equivalent to 15 soccer fields!

30

ARCHITECT: CÉSAR PELLI

(2006–2014) **8 YEARS** OF CONSTRUCTION

**SANTIAGO CHILE**

## NAVY BUILDING

31

**5 FLOORS**

**86,000 FT²**

**VALPARAÍSO CHILE**

(1907–1910) **3 YEARS** OF CONSTRUCTION

ARCHITECT: ERNESTO URQUIETA

Originally, this building was meant to be the president's summer house. After the military coup in 1973, though, the Chilean navy took possession of it and still occupies it to this day.

## NAVE TIERRA

34 The house that is self-sufficient in energy

BUILT USING **RECYCLED MATERIALS**

**333 TIRES 3,000 CANS 8,000 BOTTLES**

**THIS HOUSE WAS BUILT BY 75 PEOPLE IN 25 DAYS!**

ARCHITECT: MICHAEL REYNOLDS

2014 YEAR OF CONSTRUCTION

**USHUAIA ARGENTINA**

## THE OBELISK

**220 FT TALL** base of **527 FT²**

STAIRS WITH **206 STEPS**

36

ARCHITECT: ALBERTO PREBISCH

1936 YEAR OF CONSTRUCTION

**BUENOS AIRES ARGENTINA**

ARCHITECT: SANTIAGO CALATRAVA

2001 DATE OF INAUGURATION

**BUENOS AIRES ARGENTINA**

## PUENTE DE LA MUJER

Women's Bridge

**525 FT LONG**

The leaning mast is **111 FEET TALL** and pivots.

35

**SWING BRIDGE AT 90°** to let boats go by